THE LIFE OF EDWARD IRVING

Fore-runner of the Charismatic Movement

THE LIFE OF EDWARD IRVING

Fore-runner of the Charismatic Movement

Arnold Dallimore

THE BANNER OF TRUTH TRUST

THE BANNER OF TRUTH TRUST
3 Murrayfield Road, Edinburgh EH12 6EL
PO Box 621, Carlisle, Pennsylvania 17013, USA

*

© Arnold Dallimore 1983
First published 1983
ISBN 0 85151 369 7

*

Set in 10/12 Sabon and printed and bound at
The Camelot Press Ltd, Southampton

Contents

Contents

Illustrations

Who was Edward Irving and why this Book about him?

Edward Irving was a Presbyterian minister who served in London from 1822 till his death in 1834.

But he could also be termed a Pentecostal.

That is, during his last five years his doctrinal position was virtually that of the Pentecostal body of today. He believed God was then granting a restoration of the Apostolic gifts, especially those of 'tongues,' 'healing' and 'prophecy', and his views were such that, although he preceded our day by a century and a half, he well deserves the recognition he has recently begun to receive: 'The fore-runner of the Charismatic Movement'.

*   *   *

This man will richly repay any and all attention we may give him.

This is true, first, when we consider him in the extraordinary qualities of his person and character. He was exceptionally tall and elegantly handsome; his mind was that of a genius, though tending towards eccentricity; his spirit was almost childlike in its simplicity, yet at the same time mightily masculine, full of courage and unflinching in conviction, and as a preacher he was known as 'the greatest orator of the age'.

Here, indeed, was a most extraordinary and fascinating figure and in these pages the effort is made to present him in his rare magnificence and with warm reality.

*   *   *

Secondly, the study of Irving will prove valuable today because of his Charismatic beliefs.

The sheer facts of Irving's life in this regard are full of significance. I endeavour to show the manner in which he came into these beliefs and to portray 'the gifts in action' in his Church. Likewise I report the disappointments he faced from the 'tongues' and 'prophecies', and his story culminates in the account of the failure of his own long expectancy of being healed and the sorrow of his untimely death. And these facts are presented in a manner, I trust, which simply allows them to speak for themselves.

I have tried to write as an historian. I recognize that this book may be read by many who hold and cherish the Charismatic beliefs and I assure such persons that although my own view differs widely from that of Irving, they will here find no scoffing remark or unkind word. I have done my best to fulfil the historian's function of writing without bias and of presenting historic truth with honesty and accuracy, and I trust that to readers of all persuasions the sincerity of my effort may be apparent.

Truly, Irving's life provides much more than a fascinating account from the past – it contains warnings and instructions for the present and may well serve as a guide in one of the most important matters facing evangelical Christians today.

Arnold Dallimore   January 1983
Cottam, Ontario, Canada.

Acknowledgments

I express my heartfelt thanks to the following persons:

Mr. Gordon R. Sayer, of the Evangelical Library, London, England, for the loan of several books related to Edward Irving.

Dr. G. A. Adams, of the Toronto Baptist Seminary, for the loan of *Irving's Works*.

The Rev. L. K. Tarr, of Toronto, for the gift of Irving's *Orations*.

The Rev. Richard Owen Roberts, of Wheaton, Illinois, for the use of his extensive Bibliography on Irving.

The Rev. Iain Murray, of the Banner of Truth Trust, for copies of several original pieces of Irving's correspondence.

I am also grateful to the many friends who first urged me to write a life of Irving and who have continued to express their assurance of the need of such a work at this present time.

A Word on Special Source Material

Throughout this book the reader will find two authors cited with noticeable frequency.

One is Thomas Carlyle, a name prominent in English literature. Carlyle and Irving were close acquaintances from their teens onward, and several letters between the two men and numerous other references to Irving are to be found in Carlyle's Correspondence. Moreover, following Irving's death, Carlyle wrote a work he termed *Reminiscences*, 137 pages of which he devoted to his remembrances of Irving. Many references to this material will be found in the following pages.

The other author is a less known person – Mrs. Margaret Oliphant. Some twenty years after Irving's death this Scottish writer produced a detailed and thoroughly researched account of his life. Although her style is heavy by today's standards her volume remains by far the best biography of Irving ever written and from it the present author has gained much information and makes numerous citations.

Thomas Carlyle: *Reminiscences*. First published 1881. Present Edition published by J. M. Dent and Sons, 1972

Mrs. Oliphant: *The Life of Edward Irving*. First published, London, 1862

PART ONE

THE UPWARD-MOVING
CAREER

1792–1828

Mrs. Irving was attending a social event with other ladies in a neighbour's home one afternoon, when there came a knock upon the door.

The visitor proved to be little Edward Irving and he was insistent that he be allowed to see his mother. She went to the door and found he had met a sick boy his own age who was sorely in need of better clothes and he was strong in his request that he be allowed to give the lad some of his own.

Mrs. Irving assented to the request and the delighted Edward rushed home to supply the wants of his needy friend.

And this deed of his boyhood days was typical of many an action throughout all the years of his manhood.

I

A Happy Boyhood

In the late 1780's, Gavin Irving, a young man of the town of Annan in south-west Scotland, married Mary Lowther, a girl from a neighbouring parish.

As he brought his bride to Annan he had much reason to be proud of her. Tall, erect and shapely, her head crowned with a richness of coal-black hair, her eyes dark and lively, her speech fluent and pleasant, she was an attractive young woman indeed. And on this occasion she seemed all the more striking by reason of the red riding skirt and white Leghorn hat that she wore.

Gavin, however, was a more ordinary individual. He is described as 'a tallish man of rugged countenance, honest-hearted, rational . . .', and although not outstanding in any way, he nevertheless possessed many good qualities and much solidness of character.

The union probably brought together two blood lines of rare quality, for the Lowthers are said to have descended from Martin Luther, and some earlier generations of the Irvings had come from Huguenot stock.

Gavin and Mary settled down to a peaceful life together and as the years passed they witnessed the birth of eight children — five daughters and three sons. The second son, born 4 August, 1792, they named 'Edward'.

The Irving home was a happy one. Gavin operated a tannery business, and though it did not make him rich, it did enable him to provide his family with a relatively comfortable life. He also set the example of wholesome conduct and regular attendance at the Presbyterian Church.

Mary, however, was the guiding spirit in the home. Carlyle speaks of her as 'thrifty, assiduous, wise . . . an excellent house mother . . . full of affection and tender anxiety for her children and husband'.[1] She also possessed a natural refinement and this, by both inheritance and instruction, she passed on to her children, thereby raising them to standards of taste and manners superior to those commonly found around them.

*   *   *

Throughout his boyhood Edward was unusually tall and strong. He came by this exceptional growth naturally, for his forebears, especially on his father's side, had been notably large of stature, one uncle having been known as 'the friendly giant of the district'.

This tendency in Edward was aided by the fact that the area in which he grew up provided abundant opportunity for physical activity. It challenged a boy with its open countryside, its hills to climb, valleys to explore and an arm of the sea in which to swim. From his earliest days Edward delighted in the outdoor life and became 'distinguished for feats of swimming, walking, rowing and climbing'. He was much taller and stronger than other lads his age, and his athletic skill was accompanied by a constant vivacity of spirit – an exuberance of such a nature that when striding, as he often did, along country lanes, he could not refrain from leaping over any gate that stood in his way.

Physically, however, he suffered an unfortunate drawback. This was a misfocus of the eyes, which, while in no way affecting his sight, marred an otherwise exceptionally handsome appearance.

*   *   *

Edward's boyhood was shaped, not only by his parents but also by his school teacher, a remarkable man named Adam Hope.

Hope's methods were those of the times. He was excessively severe, frequently belittled the students and made much use of the strap. This instrument was ever in plain view – he carried it, dangling by a string from his thumb.

Hope always demanded diligent effort and drove the children to accuracy in their learning. Yet despite his severity, he achieved much success, and Carlyle states:

On Irving, who [in later years] always spoke of him with mirthful affection, he produced quietly not a little effect; prepared him well for his triumphs in Geometry and Latin at College; – and throughout life, you could always notice . . . something of that primeval logic and clear articulation laid for him in boyhood by old Adam Hope.[2]

* * *

A further influence on Edward during these formative years arose from the history of the Annandale district.

Since it was near the border which separates Scotland from England it had been at the centre of much of the warfare between the two nations. Old fortifications in a ruined condition still dotted the countryside and the area was alive with tales of their use. Many traditions of the heroism displayed by Scottish Covenanters also lingered in this area as, despite privation and torture, they withstood the attempts to force upon them the practices of the Church of England.

Thus Edward grew up excited by the thought of adventure, greatly admiring heroism and holding before himself the ideal of standing for truth whatever the cost might be.

Moreover, while he was yet a lad, Edward revealed that he, too, possessed principles for which he was willing to make a sacrifice. Most of the people of Annan attended the local congregation of the Church of Scotland, but this was not the case with all. Each Sabbath morning a little company set out to walk to Ecclefechan, a village six miles away, and there they attended a separatist congregation, a Church of the Seceders.

The Seceders were a body which had resulted from a separation made some decades earlier – a separation occasioned by a stand against doctrinal and spiritual laxity which had developed within the Church. A number of Seceding Churches had then been established and during the years which followed they had done much towards maintaining doctrinal purity and keeping the Gospel alive in many parts of Scotland.

The important point, however, is that Edward Irving, when only ten or eleven years old, often took his place among this company who walked to Ecclefechan.

Some reasons for his actions are evident.

One: the minister of the Kirk at Annan, though a man of much learning, was a slave to alcohol, and the boy, by absenting himself from the Church, was undoubtedly protesting against such behaviour and expressing his conviction that the life of a minister must be characterized by righteousness.

Two: he was indicating his agreement with a conviction of the Seceders. He was saying that to sacrifice one's ease – in this case the convenience of the Church at Annan – and to bear with difficulty the long walk in all weathers to the Ecclefechan Church – was better than injuring one's conscience in a matter of right and wrong.

But there was possibly a third and more important reason for Edward's action.

Carlyle says that throughout Scotland 'any man who awoke to the belief that he actually had a soul to be saved or lost' was likely to have left the National Church and to be found attending a congregation of the Seceders. The minister at Ecclefechan, the Rev. John Johnstone, was a man of God and there can be no doubt that the differentiating between 'saved' and 'lost' was a fundamental element of his preaching.

Accordingly the question arises, How fully did the boy become concerned about his soul? Did he, in these early years, come into a true experience of conversion?

Sad to say, there is nothing in the record to give us a clear answer to these important enquiries.

*   *   *

Nevertheless, by the time he was twelve Edward had developed a definite aim in life: he wanted to become a minister.

His boyhood had well fitted him for the preparation required for such a calling. We have seen his essential characteristics – his remarkable physique, robust health, alert mind, exuberant spirit and religious principles. These qualities constituted an excellent endowment with which to enter upon the years of study now lying between him and his cherished goal – the goal which loomed before him as the most weighty and worthy profession possible to any Scottish youth –the ministry of the National Church, the Church of Scotland.

Students were sent to Edinburgh ... when they were mere boys. ... They had no one to look after them either on their journey or when they came to the end. They walked from their homes, being unable to pay for their coach-hire.

They entered their own names at the college. They found their own humble lodgings, and were left entirely to their own capacity for self-conduct.

JAMES ANTHONY FROUDE
Thomas Carlyle: The First Forty Years of His Life, 1882

2

Teen-aged University Student

At the age of thirteen Edward left home. He and his brother John, aged fifteen, set out for Edinburgh and there they entered the University, John to study medicine and Edward to prepare for the ministry. The life before these lads in this first experience away from home was not an easy one.

Unable to afford anything better, they obtained as their lodging 'a loft in the old town'. There they lived, made their own meals – usually little more than porridge and cheese – and looked after themselves in everything.

Had the Irvings lived today they would undoubtedly have distinguished themselves in all manner of athletics. But the Universities of those days had no athletic programmes and these youths, long used to vigorous sport and open fields, now found themselves confined to crowded classrooms, busy streets and the loft in a shabby lodging house.

Moreover, they were no longer under the watchful eye of their parents. Though still so young they were on their own, yet around them lay the multiplied temptations of life in a great city.

Thus we may be sure the young Irvings often longed for home – for Annandale's open spaces, for the accustomed sporting activity and, above all, for their mother's cooking.

Furthermore, it was necessary that under these conditions they carry on a stiff academic course. Students received no personal assistance from the professors, and each must discipline himself to a stern management of his time and rigorous discipline in study –either that, or failure. And Edward, so highly vivacious and yet so young, must surely have found this programme severely trying.

Nevertheless, he benefited now from the training received under Adam Hope. He proved a good, probably an exceptional, student and was particularly successful in Mathematics, Geography, Latin and Chemistry. He became active in a kind of debating society and gave evidence of possessing, like his mother, an easy fluency of speech.

*   *   *

Edward also revealed a particular taste in literature. This matter is important as it affords us a special insight into his character and into his actions when later he began to preach.

In his personal reading he delighted in authors who used grand language and rich, rolling phrases. In this regard he read some of the great writers from the Puritan age, not so much for what they had to say as for the manner in which they said it. He carried with him a pocket edition of Ossian, an author who, though meagre in thought, was flamboyant in style. But above all, he revelled in Milton, enjoying his power and beauty, memorizing portions especially of *Paradise Lost* and repeating them as though he was playing a role on a stage.

Yet he delighted also in a totally different kind of literature. He read such works as *Don Quixote* and *Tales From The Arabian Nights*. There was in his make-up a strongly romantic element – undoubtedly also inherited from his mother – a longing for the exotic and adventurous, and he found a partial fulfilment in the excitement arising from these books.

But his use of these two forms of literature was not merely for the sake of entertainment. Rather, he regarded it as an important element in his preparation for preaching.

He had developed the idea that most ministers were dull and their sermons boring. But *he* would be different – he would use powerful, stirring language and rich rolling phrases like these favoured authors. Moreover, he believed that the life of a minister, instead of the usual colourless monotony, ought to abound in excitement, and though this was not the same kind as that of the *Arabian Nights*, it should be no less abundant and thrilling.

*   *   *

At the end of four years in the University Edward graduated. He received the Master of Arts degree, earned prizes and won the special commendations of two of his professors, Sir John Leslie and

Professor Christison. His academic record was a worthy one and his moral record unblemished.

He was now seventeen. With the passing of the years he had grown to a height of some six feet and with the increase in height there had come also a corresponding increase in muscular strength.

Shortly after graduating Edward paid a visit to his old teacher, Adam Hope at the Academy in Annan. Thomas Carlyle was a student there at the time, and several years later, looking back on the event, he wrote:

I remember to have felt some human curiosity and satisfaction when the noted Edward Irving . . . [Mr.] Hope escorting – introduced himself in our Latin classroom . . .

He was scrupulously dressed; black coat, ditto tight pantaloons in the fashion of the day . . . and looked very neat, self-possessed and enviable. A flourishing slip of a youth, with coal-black hair, swarthy clear complexion, very straight on his feet, and except for the glaring squint alone, decidedly handsome.

. . . the talk was all about Edinburgh, of this professor and of that . . . ('wonderful world up yonder, and this fellow has been in it and can talk of it in that easy cool way'.)[1]

'Scrupulously dressed . . . decidedly handsome . . . straight on his feet . . . talking in that easy cool way' – this was Edward Irving at the age of seventeen.

Irving was dowered with the double curse of originality and independence – a wayward genius, and an obstinate habit of 'standing on his own instincts'. He had fed his soul with the words of Chrysostom . . . of Jeremy Taylor . . . and of Hooker . . . till he had come to regard, as of mean speech and feeble thought, all living preachers, with the exception of Chalmers.

He had nurtured his ardent spirit by the companionship of those great churchmen . . . till he had become of such heroic mood as to disdain the timid bearing of his contemporaries . . . and despise the low arts by which, in the Scottish scarce less than in the English Establishment, the clergy obtained preferment.

WASHINGTON WILKS
Edward Irving: An Ecclesiastical and
Literary Biography, London, 1854

3

The Hard Road to the Ministry

Although Irving had completed the course in Arts there still lay before him the course in Divinity.

For this he became 'a partial student'. He taught school to support himself, did the prescribed studies under his own management and made periodic visits to the University to take the required examinations. Under this arrangement the course would take six years.

*   *   *

He was eighteen when he began to teach and his first school was in the town of Haddington.

Two matters from his days at Haddington stand out.

The first concerns the occasion when, having learned that the great Doctor Chalmers was to preach in Edinburgh he set out to walk to the city to hear him, a round trip of thirty-five miles. He took with him a group of the boys from his school.

Arriving at the church weary from their journey, teacher and pupils made their way to the gallery and went to sit down in an empty pew. Their passage, however, was blocked by an officious usher who placed his arm across the entrance to the pew and refused to let the party be seated. Irving repeatedly asked that they be allowed entrance but all entreaties failed. At last, drawing himself up to his full towering height and manifesting his strength, he thundered, 'Remove that arm, or I'll shatter it to pieces!' Needless to say, he and the boys immediately had their pew!

*   *   *

The other matter which stands out from his days at Haddington was a sparkingly happy association – his tutoring of a very exceptional little girl.

Haddington's chief physician, Dr. Welsh, asked Irving to give special instruction to his nine-year-old daughter, Jane. The lessons were given at the Doctor's home, before school began in the morning and after it had closed in the late afternoon.

Jane proved an unusually intelligent, high spirited, yet deeply sensitive youngster. Sweetly feminine, sometimes pert and independent, but always vivacious , she was a scintillating little personality.

And, of course, it was soon apparent that despite the difference in ages, student and tutor were very much alike in nature. The similarity was sensed by each and a warm affection developed.

To Irving it was merely a natural fondness for a brilliant youngster whom he termed 'My dear and lovely pupil'. But to Jane it became something more. In her childish fancy she looked up to her gigantic and chivalrous tutor with the greatest admiration. She regarded him as knowing everything and he so captivated her mind that by the time he left Haddington, she declared herself, though not yet twelve years old, 'passionately in love with him'. Of course, such words from a child usually carry little weight, but in this case they were not meaningless, for Jane was highly precocious and very mature for her age.

Moreover, although with his departure the immediate relationship ceased, the affection did not die. As we shall see, the acquaintance was renewed some eight years later when she had become a highly attractive young woman, at which time it blossomed into what was probably the deepest love Irving was ever to know.

*   *   *

Irving remained at Haddington merely two years.

By that time his unusual methods and exceptional success as a teacher had won him such a reputation that when a new school was opened at Kirkcaldy – one that was intended as a superior institution –he was asked to become the Master.

The task was a large one, especially for a youth only twenty years old. He was told the academic standards must be maintained at a level higher than that of the local parish school and that he

The Hard Road to the Ministry

was responsible to ensure that the children made rapid progress in their studies.

The schools of those days were usually places of boredom, but under his hand the Kirkcaldy Academy became a scene of lively activity and enjoyment. Like Adam Hope, he drove the children to both diligence and accuracy, although he too made far too much use of the strap. He frequently took the class out into the fields where he instructed them in the workings of nature or led them in vigorous sports. Sometimes he assembled the school again in the evening to study the heavenly bodies in the night sky, and some of the children had so exalted an opinion of their gigantic teacher that when, on two occasions, falling stars were seen, they thought some power on his part had drawn the stars towards the earth.

*   *   *

Soon, however, a third school was established in Kirkcaldy. It met in a building next door to the Academy and between the two institutions there was a rivalry which seemed likely to become bitter.

And this new school acquired as its Master a youth then unknown, but who was later to become very famous – Thomas Carlyle. This was Carlyle's first experience as a teacher. He was three years younger than Irving, and he feared that because of the hard feelings between the two schools Irving might treat him shabbily.

But he soon discovered his error. He found Irving a man entirely free from such vices as jealousy and envy, a man overflowing with goodness and charity. For instance, Irving possessed several books not then easily available in Kirkcaldy and these he invited Carlyle to use just as though they were his own. To a man of Carlyle's thirst for knowledge this was a magnificent boon and he later stated that the foundations of his love of history were laid during these hours in Irving's library.

This was the beginning of a friendship which, despite many differences of opinion, lasted throughout life and which caused Carlyle, following Irving's death, to speak of him as 'the noblest, largest, brotherliest man I have ever known'. We shall see much more of this friendship as our narrative progresses.

*   *   *

While at Kirkcaldy Irving established also another friendship – one which had a most profound effect upon his entire later career.

He became a frequent visitor to the Presbyterian manse, the home of the Rev. John Martin.

He was attracted there, however, not only by a desire for fellowship with an experienced minister, but also by a liking for the minister's eldest daughter, Isabella. He remained in Kirkcaldy another six years and during that time the relationship between himself and Isabella continued; and although there was no actual engagement, marriage was undoubtedly his intention.

And Isabella, unlikely anywhere to find a man even comparable with the magnificent Irving, gladly accepted his friendship, her thought being that he would marry her as soon as his circumstances made it possible for him to do so.

*　　　*　　　*

Irving completed his extra-mural University course in the stipulated six years and soon received his 'licence to preach'. This, however, was not ordination – it merely allowed him to preach when asked to do so by a minister and to 'make trial and proof of his gifts' with a view to being called to a church.

But some years were to elapse before Irving received such a call and the very delay reveals something highly important about Irving's character.

The Church of Scotland was then subject to the patronage system. That is, in most instances a call to a church was at the disposal of certain influential persons and much servile attention was usually paid them in seeking their favour.

This system was one of the evils the Seceders had fought against and Irving possessed too much of the same spirit to submit to it now. Moreover, he esteemed the ministry too highly to degrade it by flattering some infidel squire or fawning before an unbelieving village council, and he determined to wait, no matter how long it might take, till he received a call on his own merits.

Accordingly, he continued to teach school and he also preached from time to time.

His attempts at preaching, however, left much to be desired. He revealed an easy fluency of speech and a force of utterance, but instead of being himself and speaking naturally, he tried to be something exceptional and endeavoured to speak in the style of the great authors he had read and idolized. He used high-sounding language and rich, rolling phrases, and though some hearers delighted in his manner, most of them heartily disliked it. In fact, whenever he appeared in the pulpit the Kirkcaldy baker 'kicked his pew door open and bounced forth out of the church' and the feeling of many was expressed by the old lady who declared, 'He has ower muckle gran-ner!' ('Too much grandeur!')

* * *

By the time he had been in Kirkcaldy seven years and had reached the age of twenty-six, Irving was utterly weary of teaching school and equally tired of waiting for a call. Thus he resigned his school and moved to Edinburgh. There he did further University work, supporting himself by tutoring students and preaching whenever he had the opportunity.

But he especially made a point of hearing the Edinburgh preachers, with the result that he became still stronger in his belief that the pulpits of the land were weak and their occupants dull. All seemed to follow the wearisome old paths in both doctrine and practice and to be painfully lacking in innovation and liveliness. At the same time he felt within himself an unquenchable vitality and the surge of boundless new ideas, and he longed for the day when he would be able to put his powers to use and thereby show the ministers how the great task ought to be done.

But again the months went by and no call came.

Sorely frustrated, Irving thought of becoming a missionary to some foreign land. Such labour on some primitive shore would provide an outlet for all his pent-up energies and could also be fraught with danger and excitement – conditions without which his life seemed lacking and his soul unsatisfied. But nothing came of the missionary idea and his frustration continued.

* * *

Suddenly, however, a new light shone into Irving's life; he learned that Jane Welsh was in Edinburgh.

Jane, now a young woman of eighteen was attending finishing school. The intervening years had seen her mature both physically and intellectually and she had become an unusual specimen of youthful feminine beauty. One of her friends, a Miss Jewsbury, said of her,

... she was extremely pretty; a graceful and beautifully formed figure, upright and supple; a delicate complexion of creamy white with a pale rose-tint in the cheeks, lovely eyes full of fire and softness, and with great depths of meaning.

Her head was finely formed, with a noble arch and a broad forehead . . . . Her voice was clear and full of subtle intonations and capable of great variety of expression. She had it under full control.

She danced with much grace and was a good musician. She was ingenious in all works that required dexterity of hand; she could draw and paint and was a good carpenter. She could do anything well to which she chose to give herself.

She was fond of logic . . . and she had a clear incisive faculty of seeing through things, and hating all that was make-believe or pretentious. She had good sense that amounted to genius . . . was always witty with a gift of narration . . . Every man who spoke to her for five minutes felt impelled to make her an offer of marriage! From which it resulted that a great many men were made unhappy.'[1]

Of course, Irving immediately renewed the friendship with Jane and, as was to be expected, soon found himself falling in love.

And Jane's feelings for him were the same.

He too was an extraordinary specimen of humanity. By this time he had reached his full height – said to have been some six feet four – and since the average height was then three inches or so shorter than today, he stood out head and shoulders above the crowd. He had a flair for colourful and fashionable clothing and invariably carried himself in an erect but easy manner and his whole person had about it a lofty elegance and splendour.

And particularly noticeable was the exotic, romantic element – an indefinable quality which seemed to suggest adventure and excitement and almost gave the feeling he could just have stepped out of the *Arabian Nights*.

Even the misfocus of his eyes was not entirely a hindrance. In fact, some people found it gave his countenance a somewhat mesmerizing effect, and Crabbe Robinson, a contemporary writer, after speaking of Irving as especially attractive to the opposite sex, went on to state:

It was a question with the ladies whether his squint was a grace or a deformity. My answer would have been, 'It enhances the effect either way.'[2]

All in all, Irving was a striking figure, an example of manhood at its physical, mental and moral best.

Later developments make it evident that Irving and Jane now experienced for each other an affection which was deep and strong.

But before long, with her schooling completed, she returned to Haddington. Thereafter the relationship was maintained by correspondence, and some of Irving's letters which are extant today contain expressions of a heartfelt love.

Under these circumstances Irving was sorry he had allowed the friendship with Isabella Martin to continue so long. He hoped to be able to break it off, that he might be free to pursue the association with Jane to his heart's content.

*   *   *

Finally, however, Irving learned he was being considered for a call.

The great Doctor Chalmers, minister of St. John's Church, Glasgow, was in need of an assistant and had arranged to be present at a service in Edinburgh at which Irving was to preach.

Irving preached and seemed fairly satisfied, both with the sermon and its delivery. The minister of the church expressed his approval, as did also many of the people. But Chalmers said nothing, and went his way.

Irving waited for several days, hoping to hear from him, but no word came.

Then, unable to bear the suspense any longer, he decided to get away from it all for a time by taking passage on a vessel which would carry him down the west coast toward his native Annan. But at the last moment he changed his mind and boarded a vessel bound for northern Ireland.

As he stepped ashore in Ireland, however, he met trouble. The police were on the alert for a certain criminal and noticing Irving's gigantic build, dashing manner and mass of coal-black hair, they arrested him, feeling sure he was their man. Providentially, a local minister was able to identify him and thereby secured his release.

Still too excited to remain inactive Irving struck off, moving in his accustomed great strides, across the country. Some days later, however, upon calling at a certain post office he received a letter from his father and enclosed with it there was a note from Chalmers.

The note was favourable. It asked him to come to Glasgow for an interview.

Of course, he took the first vessel sailing for Scotland and as soon as possible sat down with Chalmers who quickly satisfied himself as to Irving's suitability and invited him to become his assistant.

Thus, at last the long wait was over.

The year was 1819, Irving was now twenty-seven, and more than fourteen years had passed since as a boy of thirteen he had left home to prepare for the ministry. It has been a long and trying road, yet even now he was not a minister in the full sense of the word – merely an assistant – but assistant to the most celebrated man in the whole of Scotland, the good and great Doctor Thomas Chalmers.

In character Dr. Chalmers possessed the virtues of his race: balance of judgment, caution combined with vehemence when aroused, sturdy honesty, strength of will and high moral aims. He had some consciousness of his powers and inclined to imperiousness, but there was also a genuine humility of soul before God. . . .

In the family circle, among friends, and in society Chalmers was a genial and lovable man, notwithstanding his strength and decisiveness. . . .

He was terribly in earnest but not self-seeking, impetuous but thoughtful, strong, wise, trustworthy and pure.

EDWIN C. DARGAN
A History of Preaching, 1904

4

Assistant to Doctor Chalmers

One of Irving's first actions upon undertaking his new duties was that of outfitting himself with new clothes. He must now be more clerically attired, the colourful fashionable garb must go, and we can imagine the lofty figure as it took on an added measure of stateliness by reason of some ministerial greys and blacks.

Nevertheless, the dashing, exciting element was not hidden. 'He looks like a brigand chief!' said one woman, while another declared 'He maun be a Highland Chief!' 'Is that Dr. Chalmers' helper?' asked a man on the street; 'I took him for a cavalry officer!' And Chalmers remarked, 'At least they all think of him as a leader of men.'

*   *   *

We may gain some further understanding of Irving as we see him in contrast with Dr. Chalmers.

First, the two men were very dissimilar physically. Irving's tall and imposing figure stood out dominantly in comparison with that of Chalmers, for Chalmers' height was merely average and his appearance, either in or out of the pulpit, was in no way attractive.

The two men were also very different in personality. Chalmers was the Christian statesman. Though his heart was ever evangelically warm, his mind was often absorbed with the problems of applying Christianity on a nation-wide scale and he could appear occupied and reserved. Irving, however, was uninhibited and open and his nature had in it much that was childlike and uncomplicated.

Chalmers' natural bent was for the solid, steady, well-proven things of life, while Irving had a flair for the spectacular, the sensational and the things which provoked excitement.

Chalmers was calm and cautious and came to a decision only after careful consideration. But Irving was often moved by impulse and soaring imagination and high idealism could over-rule for him the dictates of logic and reason.

Chalmers was also highly perceptive in his assessments of men. In this regard Irving was markedly different, for, in the openness and generosity of his nature, he could readily give ear to those who seemed likely to satisfy his penchant for things spectacular and exciting.

Looking back at Irving at this stage in his life it must be said his abilities were such as to give promise of an outstandingly great career. Nevertheless, because of his manifest deficiencies he was the kind of man who needed to be permanently under the eye of someone like Chalmers, or, failing that, to find a wife who, by adroit feminine manipulation would guard him from his natural pitfalls and guide him into wiser paths.

*   *   *

It was, however, in the preaching of the two men that the difference proved most evident.

When he had begun his ministry Chalmers had been in an unconverted state. During these years he addressed eloquent prayers to God as a far-off Deity and his message was that of urging on his hearers a formal religion and the benefits of education and culture.

But then there had come for him the great change.

In writing an article on 'Christianity' for an encyclopedia he had begun to learn what Christianity really is. Gradually he had recognized that he was a sinner, in need of salvation and unable to save himself, and by faith he had then seen Calvary, therewith to trust the finished work of Christ, to experience the new birth and to enter into newness of life.

From that point onward his ministry was transformed. His message became one of salvation by grace and the voice that formerly had reached only the mind, now reached the mind even more forcibly, but reached also the heart.

Irving, however, had no such message.

There is no evidence he had ever known an experience like that of Chalmers, the experience of conversion. He was, of course, a fully moral man and he preached with much earnestness, especially in his condemnation of sin. But, as Carlyle said, his message at this stage of his life was largely:

'If this thing is true, why not do it? You had better do it; there will be nothing but misery and ruin in not doing it!' – that was the gist . . . of all his discoursing.[1]

Irving made no clear statement about salvation and his preaching was not accompanied by any true power from on high.

Nevertheless, his ministry proved particularly attractive to a small portion of the congregation of St. John's, and they preferred his preaching to that of Chalmers.

But with the vast majority the response was the opposite. Many considered his preaching far too grandiose, and some would not even hear him. On more than one Sabbath morning as he approached the Church he found groups of people leaving – they had learned that he, not Doctor Chalmers, was to preach at that service and they were on their way home, complaining as they went, 'It's no himsel' the day!' No one but 'himsel' would suit them.

*   *   *

Perhaps Irving's chief work, at this period, lay in visiting the inhabitants of a poverty-stricken area of the parish – the homes of the Calton weavers.

When employed, the men of this area laboured long hours for small pay in Glasgow's weaving mills. But the installation of new machinery had recently thrown many of them out of work and as a result suffering was widespread, sickness abounded, and there was a lack of sufficient coal in the winter time.

More than once during the previous months these needy people had arisen in violent protest against their conditions. The civic officials had quelled the uprisings by force of arms, and now, fearing the breaking point was near again, they had quartered soldiers among them, armed and ready to act.

In view of this situation Chalmers had inaugurated an extensive system of immediate relief, and also of long-range changes which would effect a permanent improvement in the lives of these people.

But at the time Irving began his work, this system was in its infancy. Suffering faced him everywhere and although most pastors would have undertaken the visitation of these homes only with great reluctance, he launched into it with vigour and even with some measure of delight.

Never had these people seen such a man. As he made his way along their dreary streets he greeted everyone he met, his towering figure in its ministerial garb standing out conspicuously among the under-fed and ill-clad populace.

He called at one poor dwelling after another and at every door he pronounced the greeting, 'Peace be to this house!' Invited in, he placed his great hands on the head of each child, praying as he did so, 'The Lord bless thee and keep thee!' And he made the elderly and the sick his special concern, showing them every possible assistance and kindness.

Of course, in those days before the use of electricity or sanitation systems, conditions must have been much worse than in such districts today. Irving must often have met some very difficult situations – sights and sounds and smells which were highly obnoxious – but of such things he says nothing.

Moreover, he had a gift for making himself at home among these people. Chalmers knew and loved them *en masse* but Irving knew them individually. To him they quickly became first-name acquaintances and he spoke to Donald and Jean and Sandy and Elizabeth just as though they were his long standing friends. Sometimes, in the midst of a conversation he would walk to the grate and help himself to a potato from a pot cooking over the fire, and he often assisted some over-worked mother or struggling father in some menial household task.

During these days Irving received a small legacy – probably about £100. He changed the whole amount into £1 notes, and each morning, as he went forth to his visitation he took one of the notes with him. During the day he left the note, equal to the amount received by a weaver for nearly two weeks' work, in one of the homes, and we may be sure the deed brought as much joy to the giver as to the recipient.

An incident which occurred later (when Irving had become a minister in London) provides a beautiful picture of his relations with the poor. Some London ladies had begun a school for small children in the Billingsgate district, but were unsuccessful in persuading the mothers to let their children attend. So they turned to Irving for help.

Accordingly, he went with the ladies to Billingsgate. At the first home he listened while they went through their procedure of informing a half-frightened mother that they had chosen to help her by providing a school for her little ones. But their pompous manner repelled the mother and again they were turned away without success.

At the second house Irving took over. He introduced himself and the ladies in the kindest tone and was soon allowed entrance. There he graciously explained the purpose of the ladies, talked about the school and asked the mother if she would assist by allowing her children to attend. While speaking he took a little girl upon his knee, praying as usual, 'The Lord bless thee and keep thee!' And soon he won the mother's consent concerning her children's attendance at the school, and, indeed, gained her lasting goodwill.

When the party had returned to the street one of the ladies exclaimed:

Why Mr. Irving! You spoke to that woman as if she were doing *you* a favour, and not you conferring one on *her*! How could you speak so? And how could you take that child upon your knee!

But this was Edward Irving in his love for the poor, whether in Billingsgate or Glasgow, and it is to be hoped the proud ladies benefited from his example.

The visitation among the Calton weavers was Irving's chief pastoral labour during his days with Chalmers. His kindness and devotion merit our warmest praise, yet it is much to be regretted that he did not go to these people with the Gospel, thereby to see men and women converted, sin's power broken and lives transformed by grace.

*   *   *

The relationship between Irving and Chalmers, though always cordial, was never fully satisfactory to either of them.

Chalmers was frequently – perhaps constantly – concerned lest Irving should do or say something too extreme, something erratic which would cause problems.

And Irving was not happy in being merely an assistant. He felt the inferiority of his position and disliked standing in Chalmers' shadow. He was not cut out for a secondary figure, for his mind teemed with ideas, he knew he possessed exceptional abilities and his ambitions ran very high. Yet his immense powers were largely unused till he could become the minister of a congregation of his own – a minister in the full function of that office.

Under the daily experience of this discontent Irving again thought of becoming a missionary. But before he came to a decision his prospects were altered; he received two letters each enquiring as to his willingness to be considered for a call – one from a large congregation in Jamaica and the other from a highly prestigious church in New York.

And while these letters were before him he received also another. This proved to be all-important – the communication on which his whole future turned.

The Caledonian Chapel in London was without a minister and its officials invited Irving to supply for a few Sundays. He gladly complied and found his preaching so well received that he was given a virtually unanimous call to become the Chapel's minister.

Of course there was no hesitation: he quickly accepted the call. Hastening to begin his duties he soon preached a farewell sermon at St. John's, was ordained at his old home church in Annan, and then, stirred to the depths of his being by the prospects now open before him, fully confident of his powers, yet humbly seeking the help of God, he set out to undertake a ministry at the heart of the nation, the greatest city in the world: London, England.

A singular phenomenon appeared in the religious world. . . . A Presbyterian minister, then unknown to fame, came to an obscure place of worship in the metropolis and took all ranks of society by storm. . . .

He produced an excitement which, from the extent to which it prevailed, the class of persons it affected, and the prophetic fervour it displayed, rose to the importance of a national event.

DR. JOHN STOUGHTON

History of Religion in England, 1800–1850

5

The Sudden Burst into Fame

The Caledonian Chapel possessed nothing which of itself should make Irving or anyone else excited.

It was situated in the Hatton Garden district, a rather shabby area of mean houses and narrow streets. For the preceding year it had been without a pastor, the congregation had dwindled to fifty and many thought its end was near.

But to Irving the Caledonian Chapel represented the one thing he wanted – an opportunity.

The call to its pastorate made him a minister in the full sense of the word. Now he was free to chart his own course, free to use to the limit his mighty powers and free to labour in a manner suited to his own ideas and aims. For years he had longed for such circumstances that he might demonstrate to the world a ministry that was alive, innovative and adventurous – and at last the opportunity to do so was in his hands. To some people this obscure Chapel might seem a forlorn hope but to him it was an exciting challenge.

*   *   *

The opportunity proved to be all that was necessary to bring Irving's full range of abilities into action.

With joyous abandon he thrust himself into his work. He laboured in the preparation of his sermons, visited the homes of his people, and made himself available at all hours to any who sought his aid. He preached with fervour, exuded confidence and radiated vitality, and in a letter to Jane Welsh he appears as a new man:

... I have become all at once full of hope and activity. My hours of study have doubled themselves – my intellect, long unused to expand itself, is awakening again, and truth is revealing itself to my mind.[1]

Under so vital a ministry conditions at the Chapel began to change. The people were much encouraged and the attendances steadily increased, and Irving could have gone on this way, developing over the years a large congregation.

But any such gradual growth proved entirely unnecessary. When he had been in London merely six months success came to him with almost hurricane force and in tidal wave proportions.

This sudden popularity was sparked by the interest of the Honourable George Canning, one of Britain's foremost statesmen and later her Prime Minister.

Canning was told that Irving, in praying for a family of orphans, had referred to them as 'now cast upon the Fatherhood of God'. The term 'the Fatherhood of God' was something new at the time and Canning found it particularly appealing. Accordingly, he went to hear Irving for himself and a few days later, in addressing Parliament he not only mentioned Irving but described his sermon as the most eloquent he had ever heard. Thereafter Canning attended the Chapel regularly and became a most enthusiastic supporter of Irving. He daily urged his associates to join him in listening to 'the greatest orator of our times'.

Thus, tremendously helped by Canning's endorsement and constantly exercising his own magnificent powers, Irving entered upon a popularity which was utterly amazing.

Sabbath by Sabbath the Chapel which seated some 500 became a scene of tumult as twice and thrice that number sought entrance. Long before the hour of service the building was filled, every seat occupied and every aisle packed, yet even then one might see some titled gentleman jostling with a labourer for standing room in a vestibule or might observe a peeress pushing to obtain the last foot of seating space on the pulpit stairs.

Outside, the streets became impassable with the congestion of carriages, while a host of would-be hearers thronged noisily around the doors in a vain attempt to get in.

*   *   *

The congregation which thus gathered to hear Irving, though composed of people of all kinds, was particularly notable for the proportion of professional people it contained. Lawyers, physicians, actors, artists, diplomats – men from these and similar walks of life, together with their fine ladies, were drawn in large numbers to this ministry.

And among these professional hearers England's literary circles were especially well represented. On almost any Sabbath there might be seen, pressed in somewhere among the crowd, such notables as Zachary Macaulay, Charles Lamb, William Hazlitt ('who had forgot what the inside of a church was like'), Thomas De Quincey, S. T. Coleridge, together with several other literary figures who, though little known today, were prominent then. Moreover young Thomas Macaulay attended at times and Dorothy and William Wordsworth and Sir Walter Scott were present once or twice – at least often enough to form an opinion regarding Irving.

Under Canning's influence several Members of Parliament became regular hearers. And William Gladstone, writing in later life when he had become Prime Minister, told of attending the Chapel as a boy, and mentioned his mischievous delight in seeing the Head Master of Eton College 'mercilessly compressed' amidst the crush in the centre aisle, while he himself, having arrived early, sat comfortably in the front row of the gallery.

*   *   *

Of course, all manner of reports about Irving and his preaching were circulated. As was but to be expected, some were severely critical, but one of the more friendly accounts describes a Sunday morning service as follows:

Eleven o'clock strikes . . . there is a rustle, instantly succeeded by a deep silence.

Edward Irving mounts the pulpit with a measured and dignified pace. . . . His expression is very peculiar; it is not that of fear, deference, still less of impertinence, anger or contempt. It is simply the look of a man who says internally, 'I am equal to this occasion, in the dignity and power of my own intellect and nature, and MORE than equal to it in the might of my Master, and in the grandeur of my message.' . . .

He gives out a Psalm – the twenty-ninth – and as he reads it his voice seems the echo of 'the Lord's voice upon the waters', so deep and far rolling are the crashes of its sound. . . . Then he reads a portion of Scripture . . . the twenty-third Psalm, to give relief to the grandeurs that have passed or that are at hand.

Then he says, 'Let us pray', not as a mere formal preliminary, but because he really wishes to gather up all the devotional feeling of his hearers along

with his own, and present it as a whole burnt-offering to Heaven. His voice
... rises to God, and you feel as if God had blotted out the church around
and the universe above, that that voice might obtain immediate entrance to
His ear. ...

The sermon is on the days of the Puritans and the Covenanters, and his
blood boils as he fights over again the battles ... he paints the dark
muirlands, whither the Woman of the Church retired for a season to be
nourished with blood, and you seem to be listening to that wild eloquence
which pealed through the wilderness and shook the throne of Charles the
Second.

Then he turns to contrast that earnest period with 'our light, empty and
profane era' and opens with fearless hand the vials of apocalyptic wrath
against it. He speaks of 'our godless system of ethics and economics. . . .' He
attacks the poetry and criticism of the age ... and eyeing the peers and
peeresses, the orator denounces 'wickedness in high places', and his voice
swells with the deepest thunder . . . as he characterizes the false courtiers, the
hypocrisy of statesmen, the hollowness, licentiousness and levity of fashionable life.

The language is worthy of the message it conveys, not polished, indeed
rather rough ... vehement, figurative and bedropt with terrible or tender
extracts from the Bible. The manner is as graceful as may well co-exist with
deep and impetuous force ... The voice seems meant for 'an orator of the
human race' ... and to plead in mightier causes than can be conceived of in
our degenerate days.[2]

Such was Irving's ministry as viewed by one of his contemporaries.
We do well to notice that the service was characterized by a typically
Presbyterian solemnity, but also that the sermon appears to have been
largely a lecture in church history, rather than an exposition of the
Scriptures or the preaching of the Gospel.

William Hazlitt, writing as a frequent hearer, stated:

Mr. Irving's intellect is of a superior order; he has undoubtedly both talents
and acquirements beyond the ordinary run of every-day preachers. . . His
very unusual size and height are moulded into elegance by the most
admirable symmetry of form and ease of gesture; his sable locks, his clear
iron-grey complexion and firm-set features, turn the raw uncouth Scotch-
man into the likeness of a noble Italian picture.[3]

*   *   *

Several of the well-to-do families among Irving's hearers
endeavoured to make him into a social lion. He was still a single man
and they vied with one another in seeking to have him as their guest.
The home of Mr. and Mrs. Basil Montagu appears to have been
especially appealing to him. Mrs. Montagu sought to bestow on him

a motherly kind of care, and he made her his confidant in the matter of his affection for Jane Welsh. The Montagu drawing room was a gathering place of *the beau monde* and Irving acquired some further measure of culture as there he conversed with men and women of prominence in literature, music and art. Yet although he manifestly enjoyed the attentions of these people, he never allowed himself to be looked upon as merely another professional figure, but in these, as in all other associations, his conduct forced all who knew him to recognize him as a man of God.

Nevertheless, the less prominent members of his flock had the larger portion of his time. He loved the poor in London just as he had loved the poor in Glasgow and he had always a special care and concern for children and the elderly. To many people he seemed the very essence of what they felt a minister should be: with a zeal like that of an Old Testament prophet he condemned sin, especially sin in high places, and made wealthy corrupters or evil-doers in government cringe under his jeremiads; but the penitent or the suffering ever found in him a most gracious friend and he visited the sick or watched by the dying with heart-felt compassion.

*   *   *

Thus Irving passed his first year in London.

And as the year came to its close he was in a dizzying position – he stood upon the pinnacle of fame.

He was ever 'news' in the eyes of the press. Of course, some papers belittled him, and other praised him, but he could not be overlooked, and more than once some important coverage was omitted in order that space might be given to something he had said or done.

Among the public the attitude was similar. Some people considered him a cheap charlatan and others were sure he would be merely a nine-days' wonder, briefly famous and soon forgotten.

But numerous others regarded him as a true and mighty man of God and the opinion of many was similar to that expressed by De Quincey: 'Mr. Irving is, by many degrees, the greatest orator of the age!'

*   *   *

Great popularity is hard for any man to bear, and Irving found it particularly difficult.

He had come so recently out of obscurity and had been thrust so suddenly into fame, that he was at a loss as to how to meet this situation. He knew not where his success would end and moved by his soaring imagination he began to foresee his ministry ever expanding till it reached all parts of Britain and he even thought of it as growing without limit throughout the world.

Moreover, even at its best his judgment was not well-balanced, but tended towards the eccentric. And now, standing as he did at the height, he could not easily evaluate either his position or himself, and he faced the danger of far too great a measure of self-concern and self-esteem.

This was the very situation Whitefield had faced eighty years earlier and which Spurgeon was to face thirty years later. Each of these men experienced in London a fame exceeding that of Irving and each of them met it in a sense of increased dying unto self and deeper devotion to God. Whitefield cried, 'Let the name of Whitefield perish, but Christ be glorified, and let me be but the servant of all.' Spurgeon prayed that he might so set forth the Lord Jesus Christ in the power of His death that he himself might be 'hidden behind the cross' and the hearers might see only the Saviour.

But Irving was different. After the passing of some years and the experiencing of several trials he acquired a considerable humility, but during the months immediately before him, despite his many good qualities, he too easily asserted his superiority and too often made mention of his success.

Irving's sudden and unexampled popular applause did not completely turn his head, but it distinctly injured him. It left him an enthusiastic, simple-minded man; but it gave him overweening confidence in himself; and it infected him with the illusion that some high and world-wide mission had been committed to him.

B. B. WARFIELD
Counterfeit Miracles, 1918

6

Irving's Reaction to Popularity

Before leaving Scotland Irving had spoken about the aims and ambitions with which he would work in London. He wanted, he said,

to make a demonstration for a higher style of Christianity, something more magnanimous, more heroical than this age affects.[1]

To a fellow minister he asserted, 'Now you shall see what great things I will do' and when the two of them were crossing a loch in a ferry boat he stated:

You are content to go backward and forward on the same route, like this boat. But as for me, I hope yet to go deep into the ocean of truth.[2]

Irving's meaning is clear. In his opinion ministers merely repeat the same old dogmas Sunday after Sunday and seek nothing new in either doctrine or practice.

But this will not do for him!

He will not submit to the 'ferry-boat' life lived by other men. He sees before him a virtual ocean and he is resolved both to sail in its breadth and to search into its depth. He will demonstrate a style of Christianity higher and more heroic than the kind seen elsewhere – indeed, he will shew the ministers what great things he can do and will present an example of how the ministry ought to be conducted.

*　　　*　　　*

Irving revealed his assurance that he had accomplished these aims, when, at the beginning of his second year in London, he published his first book.

The book is in two parts: *For the Oracles of God: Four Orations* and *For Judgment to Come: An Argument.*

In the *Preface* Irving asserts that the people of England and Scotland are ignorant of the basic truths of Christianity and that this ignorance results, not from lack of interest on their own part but from 'the want of a sedulous and skilful ministry'. He charges that the preaching of the ministers is suited to the lower classes of mankind. 'They prepare men for teaching gipsies, for teaching bargemen, for teaching miners,' he says, and he asks '. . . why not train ourselves for teaching imaginative men and political men, and legal men and medical men?' and the inference is that this is the class he has attracted in London.

He accuses the ministers of failing to preach in a manner plainly understandable by their people, and then declares:

. . . I have set the example of two new methods of handling religious truth – *the Oration* and *the Argument*; the one intended to be after the manner of the ancient Oration, the best vehicle for addressing the minds of men . . . far beyond the sermon, of which the very name hath learned to inspire drowsiness and tedium; the other after the manner of the ancient Apologies, with this difference, that it is pleaded, not before any judicial bar, but before the tribunal of human thought and feeling.[3]

Thus, even in the *Preface* Irving flaunts his success.

Other ministers preach sermons – the method of 'drowsiness and tedium' – but *he* delivers Orations, 'after the manner of the ancient Apologies'. *He* makes use of Argument and the inference is that the reasoned form of presentation is not employed by other preachers.

It was true his methods had proved highly successful but it was unseemly for him to contrast himself with others in this way.

*   *   *

Nevertheless, despite his success as a preacher, throughout the book Irving is far from successful as an author.

Granted, page after page is characterized by vigorous language and powerful imagination and a style which is so much out of the ordinary that it frequently suggests genius.

But at the same time there is such a straining after grandeur, such a display of an ability to create rolling phrases and to use ornate diction that the book is very hard to read and its message almost impossible to ascertain. Irving had impregnated his mind with the flamboyancies of Ossian and the sublimities of Milton and had tried to make them his own, but he would have done far better had he copied, for instance, such down-to-earth writers as Flavel and Bunyan.

The book brought Irving criticism – some good and some bad. Because of his prominence it went through three editions in four months. But the attitude of many readers was like that of Carlyle who, after praising parts of it, stated that much of the book, because of its unnatural style and pompous wordiness, made him laugh out loud while he read it.

The reaction of many readers was similar and some stated that although they had previously believed Irving's spirit to be proud, that his mind lacked adequate balance and that he was an unprincipled opportunist who would do anything to gain popularity, the book now proved that those suspicions were true.

*   *   *

There can be little doubt that Irving would have been far wiser to have published nothing at this stage of his career. Despite the fact that he was now thirty years old he was yet immature and it was his inexperience combined with his native penchant for self-display which caused him to act in this fashion.

Nevertheless, he was a much better man than his manner of behaviour sometimes suggested. Though he had this tendency to boastfulness he also possessed much real lowliness of heart. He delighted in his fame but at the same time he was governed by high principles and he would not alter them one iota to please any man on earth.

*   *   *

While the publication of Irving's first book increased the number of those who belittled him, there were still a great many who admired the preacher and author. And this wide adulation made it evident that the number of those who thronged together every Sunday to hear him would always far exceed the seating capacity of the Caledonian Chapel. Therefore the Trustees were already making plans toward the construction of a new church – a magnificent edifice capable of seating 1,800 or more and worthy in its architectural quality to take its place as the National Scotch Church in London.

Edward Irving

Admittedly Irving had his adversaries and his weaknesses, but as he looked out upon the days before him his prospects were magnificently bright – yea, he could see little that was not inviting and glorious.

With the new building rising on its site in Regent Square, Irving wrote to his wife who was away from home:

I walked melancholy enough along Burton Crescent to see the church for the second time, which is now up to the level of the first windows, indeed above it; and in front the yellow stones are showing themselves above the ground, and when it is finished I doubt not it will be a seemly building. But may the Lord fill it with the glory of His own spiritual presence, and endow me with gifts to watch over the thousands who are to assemble therein, or raise up some one more worthy and take me to His rest.

It would seem that in the extreme spiritual vicissitudes of his life Coleridge at times threw himself entirely on the consolations of evangelical faith, and at others reconstructed the cosmos for himself in terms of Neo-Platonism and the philosophy of Schelling.

So great were his variations even in his latter years, that he could speak to his friend Allsop in a highly latitudinarian sense, declaring that in Christianity 'the miracles are supererogatory', and that 'the law of God and the great principles of the Christian religion would have been the same had Christ never assumed humanity'.

The Encyclopedia Britannica, 1909 ed.
Article, 'Coleridge, S. T.'

7

A Unique Friendship: Irving and Coleridge

We have seen that one of the regular attendants at Irving's services was England's celebrated critic, poet and philospher: Samuel Taylor Coleridge.

This was an unexpected development.

During his early manhood Coleridge had held to Unitarian views – basically a denial of the deity of Christ. He also began to use alcohol and narcotics, at first as a means of relieving pain, but he soon indulged to excess and became enslaved. Thereby he ruined his health, his home and his career and this was the situation till, in 1815, a London physician took him into his home and by strict supervision enabled him largely to overcome his habits. But he remained a physical wreck, so deteriorated in body as to be almost repulsive.

By that time, however, having found Unitarianism powerless he had returned to the Church of England. But this was merely a nominal relationship, for he had also taken up with the transcendentalism of certain German philosophers. He rejected much of evangelical Christianity, especially the evangelical attitude towards the Scriptures, holding that the *letter* of the Bible is unimportant and often erroneous, that only the *spirit* of the Bible is trustworthy and that this alone conveys its message.

Coleridge possessed an exceptionally penetrating and retentive mind. He was highly revered in the intellectual world and many, especially the literary people, resorted to him to drink in the wisdom that flowed from his lips. To have the good will of S. T. Coleridge was considered a boon indeed.

When Irving burst into fame in London, Coleridge not only attended his preaching but became so fascinated by his oratory that he pronounced him 'The super Ciceronian, ultra Demosthenic pulpiteer.' And later he declared:

I hold that Edward Irving possesses more of the spirit and purpose of the first Reformers, that he has more of the Head and Heart, the Life, the Unction, and the genial power of Martin Luther, than any man now alive. . . .[1]

Irving was highly flattered by Coleridge's attentions and became deeply attached to him. Admiring him as the supreme philosopher he visited him often and sat at his feet to hear his words of wisdom.

More than once he took Carlyle on these visits. But Carlyle regarded Coleridge more as a warning against dissipation than a teacher to be revered. He described him as 'a puffy, fattish, hobbling old man', and went on to say,

Good Irving strove always to think he was getting priceless wisdom out of this great man, but he must have had his misgivings.[2]

On one occasion Chalmers went with Irving to visit the sage. He reported:

We spent three hours with the great Coleridge. His conversation flowed in a mighty unremitting stream. . . . Irving sits at his feet, and drinks in the inspiration of every syllable. . . . There is a secret and, to me . . . unintelligible communion of spirit betwixt them, on the ground of a certain German mysticism and transcendental lake poetry which I am not yet up to.[3]

And Irving himself gave strong testimony concerning the influence Coleridge had on him. He stated he had learned more of 'orthodox doctrine' from Coleridge than from 'all the men with whom I have entertained friendship and conversation' and that from him his 'mind received a new insight into the depths of truth'.

Thus Coleridge passed on his views to Irving and in so doing he altered the course of Irving's theological thinking. This seems to be true in three very important areas.

The first concerned the person of Christ. Coleridge had never fully overcome his Unitarian beliefs and although he professed to hold the doctrines of the Church of England his concept of Christ was a hazy transcendental idea to the effect that Christ's nature was something less than divine. He does not appear to have distinguished between 'nature' and 'person' and he thus failed to assert that this Christ is 'God and man, in two distinct natures, and one person for ever'.

Irving instead of recognizing Coleridge's confusion was not alert to a danger which we shall see emerging in his own subsequent statements.

The second related to the concept of the prospects then lying before mankind. Irving had taken it for granted that the world was moving towards greater and greater Gospel triumphs – that there would soon be an era of universal blessing. But Coleridge declared the world was moving, not towards better conditions, but to worse. 'Let this young man know,' he declared, 'this world is not to be converted, but judged!' and he held that directly before mankind there lay a period of terrible suffering.

Yet Coleridge could also foresee, amidst such difficulties, the possibility of better conditions – a victory of the transcendental, a time when men might find their spiritual desires transcend their material appetites.

The third concerned the doctrine of the Holy Spirit. Coleridge held that the preacher, in performing his task, was virtually 'the voice of the Holy Spirit' – an idea he presented in the following diagram:

CHRIST = Prothesis
HOLY SPIRIT = Mesothesis
SCRIPTURE = Thesis   CHURCH = Thesis
THE PREACHER = Synthesis of
CHURCH and SCRIPTURE
'the sensible voice of the Holy Spirit'.[4]

Coleridge's influence in these things immediately became evident in Irving's preaching. The prospect of mankind's moving towards terrible judgment, but also the possibility of the transcendence of the spiritual over the material through the direct working of the Holy Spirit, had a powerful appeal for him. Here were important elements of the 'deeper truth' and 'higher style of Christianity' for which he had been seeking and with all the enthusiasm of his nature he embraced them.

*   *   *

These new beliefs influenced Irving when at this time he addressed a very important gathering and did so in a manner which shocked his hearers.

Edward Irving

Each year the officials of the London Missionary Society obtained the largest auditorium and the finest speaker available, for a great rally by which to promote their work. And during Irving's third year in London (1824) they asked him to be their speaker and they obtained as their meeting place the Whitefield Chapel in Tottenham Court Road.

They expected Irving would extol the past accomplishments of the Society, would tell of recent triumphs on the field and, after pointing out areas of particular need, in a great oratorical finale would arouse his hearers to a new devotion to the Society and to a liberal support of its work.

But before an audience which overflowed the building and in a meeting which lasted three and a half hours, Irving said the very opposite of what he was expected to say.

Entitling his address *For Missionaries after the Apostolic School* he described with great eloquence the supernatural power possessed by the Church in its first centuries. He portrayed the lives of the Apostles as characterized constantly by miracles and he spoke of the men themselves as independent of all earthly assistance and dependent solely upon God. He charged that the Church had drifted from the purity and practices of those days and that as a result she had lost her power and in her weakness had resorted to human devices and earthly organizations.

He pictured the true missionary,

... a man without staff or scrip, without banker or provision, abiding with whomsoever would receive him, speaking in haste his burning message, pressing on without pause or rest through the world that lay in wickedness – an Apostle responsible to no man – a messenger of the cross.[5]

Although he did not actually say so, Irving implied that missionary Societies were not only unnecessary but were the outcome of apostasy. Let the missionaries go out to the foreign lands without human support, let them trust God to sustain them, let all dependence on earthly organizations be abandoned, and such a return to Apostolic practice will result in a return of Apostolic power. This was his essential message.

Of course, such statements created a furor. The officials were highly incensed and denounced the address as 'visionary and wild' and as 'an implied libel on the Society', and many people declared they had always believed Irving was unbalanced and vain and that such behaviour proved the belief to be true.

But Irving did not merely deliver the address – he published it too. And to make the offence still worse he prefaced the pamphlet with a *Dedication* to none other than Coleridge. In this he assured the sage:

. . . you have been more profitable to my faith in orthodox doctrine, to my spiritual understanding of the Word of God, and to my right conception of the Christian Church, than any or all the men with whom I have entertained friendship.

. . . your many conversations concerning the revelations of the Christian faith have been so profitable to me . . . and your high intelligence and great learning have at all times so kindly stooped to my ignorance and inexperience, that . . . with the gratitude of a disciple to a wise and generous teacher, of an anxious inquirer to the good man who hath helped him in the way of truth, I do presume to offer you the first fruits of my mind since it received a new impulse towards truth, and a new insight into its depths from listening to your discourse.[6]

The offence given by the address itself was doubled by the *Dedication*. Nothing whatsoever in Coleridge's actions or writings qualified him to be addressed as an orthodox Christian, and to those who truly were orthodox Irving's statements seemed utterly ridiculous.

*   *   *

Thus it was evident Irving needed a wise counsellor in the journey of life. Chalmers would have provided the help he needed but Irving was unwilling to listen to him. But he had turned to Coleridge and his thinking had been altered by an influence which flowed in but a minor way from the Scriptures and in a major manner from human philosophy.

There remained, however, the possibility of his obtaining better guidance. This lay in the hope that he would find a suitable wife – a strong but tactful woman who would graciously warn him of his tendency to extremes and would lead him in the ways of wisdom.

There would have been no tongues if Irving had married me!

JANE WELSH CARLYLE, 1834

8

Marriage

At this stage in his life Irving was, of course, a single man and lived in rented lodgings. But he needed a home of his own and by the time he had been in London a year he had reached the age of thirty-one and was thinking of getting married.

His situation, however, was not an easy one. Although his heart moved in one direction his responsibilities forced him in another.

First, there was his association with Isabella Martin.

Twelve years earlier he had entered into a friendship with Isabella and in a typical large-hearted lack of caution had allowed it to continue. She was not physically attractive nor brilliant of mind, but she came of good stock, possessed a true integrity of character and was a woman of much practical good sense. Accordingly, Irvine took it for granted she would make a good 'manse wife'. He had never actually engaged to marry her, but during the first six years of the friendship – that is, until Jane Welsh came into his life again – marriage was undoubtedly his intention.

In turn, Isabella accepted the long friendship and relied on the implied intention. And as the years passed she looked on her relationship with Irving as 'an understanding' that they would be married and she expected the event would take place as soon as he was settled in a pastorate.

*　　　*　　　*

But much had changed for Irving when Jane Welsh re-entered his life.

Upon renewing the acquaintance with Jane – during his days in Edinburgh – he had begun to break off the relationship with Isabella. This brought the strong disapproval of both Isabella and her father.

But after becoming settled in London he became more definite in the effort to dissociate himself from Isabella. And this time she and her father declared that since he had maintained the friendship with her so long he now had no choice but to marry her.

His desires, however, moved him much more towards Jane.

Irving was a man of strong emotions, his nature cried out for excitement and he needed not only physical but also intellectual and emotional companionship. And in these areas – areas to which Isabella was largely a stranger – his thoughts and feelings were fully matched by those of Jane.

Thus Irving faced a problem. Were he to forsake Isabella after this long friendship, the action would not only be considered a blot on his character but would also bring reproach on the office of the ministry. Moreover, in the kindness which was so large a part of his nature he dreaded the thought of hurting the patient Isabella.

*　　　*　　　*

But now difficulty arose concerning Jane also.

Sometime earlier Irving had introduced Carlyle to Jane, and he, unaware of Irving's affection for her, had quickly fallen in love with her himself. Nevertheless, Jane considered Carlyle somewhat un-couth and her affection remained attached to the elegant Irving.

Jane's attitude, however, soon began to change. Carlyle was steadily drifting away from the Presbyterian beliefs and he was accepting instead the teachings of the German rationalists. And under his influence Jane likewise began to turn away from the Presbyterian tenets and increasingly accepted those of rationalism.

Of course, both she and Irving realized that such a change ruled out any possibility of their being married.

Thus they each faced a bitter decision. Despite their love for one another there could be no choice but the heart-breaking one – that of parting! She must go her way and he must go his! So they parted, Jane to continue the friendship with Carlyle and Irving to return to Isabella.

*　　　*　　　*

Isabella was certainly different from Jane. We may be sure she did not deserve the epithet Carlyle used of her, 'dead ugly', but there is likely much truth in his further comment, 'She is unbeautiful; has no enthusiasm and few ideas that are not prosaic or conceited, but possesses, I believe, many household virtues.'

Nevertheless, from the beginning Irving had experienced a considerable measure of affection for her, and now that the Jane affair was over, moved by that affection and by a sense of responsibility, he decided to marry her.

The wedding took place on 13 October, 1823, at Isabella's home in Kirkcaldy. It was followed by a honeymoon trip through southern Scotland. Upon meeting up with Carlyle, Irving invited him to accompany them for a day or two and Carlyle spoke of his friend as 'supremely happy'.

*   *   *

In London, Irving and Isabella settled down to the joys and duties of married life.

Their home seems to have been one of entire harmony, except for one difficulty. That is, although Irving and Jane had decided to part, the bonds which had entwined their hearts were not completely severed.

Jane tried to disguise her feelings by speaking meanly of Irving. In several of her letters to Carlyle she referred to him as having become big-headed and used such terms as 'the great centre of attraction, the Spanish Adonis! the reverend Edward Irving himself!' 'He has not a head for these London flatteries. . . . It will be all over with him if he forgets his earliest and best friends,' she declared.

After receiving several such letters from her, Carlyle replied:

What a wicked creature you are to make me laugh at poor Irving! Do I not know him for one of the best men breathing, and that he loves both of us as if he were our brother?[1]

The editor of Carlyle's correspondence remarks:

All of Jane's protestations and sometimes cruel fun about Irving stem from the fact that she had been in love with him. . . . Her character was profoundly affected by this early disappointment. . . . Carlyle never completely realized the intensity of the feeling that had been crushed.[2]

And Irving's feelings for Jane were also not easily overcome. Some few months after his marriage he invited her (she was not yet married) to come to London as the guest of Isabella and himself in order that she might be near Carlyle. The idea met strong opposition from Isabella, and Irving somewhat changed his own mind. More than once he wrote to Jane giving reasons why it would be unwise for her to come at that time, but finally he wrote stating the true reason – that he could not yet trust himself to have her so near. His letter reads:

One thing more, my dear Jane, into your own ear. My dear Isabella has succeeded in healing the wounds of my heart, but I am hardly yet in a condition to expose them. My former calmness and piety are returning. I feel [I am] growing in grace . . . and before another year I shall be worthy in the eye of my own conscience, to receive you into my house and under my care, which till then I shall hardly be. Be assured, my dear Jane, the child of my intellect, of the same affection from me as ever, and as I have said, pure and yet more pure.[3]

This matter of Irving's disappointment in love is important in our effort to know and understand him.

A man of his depth of emotion and his capacity for affection could not have endured this heart-breaking experience without suffering tremendously. The statement that because of it 'he flung himself into religious excitement as grosser natures go into drink' is false, but at the same time there can be no doubt he was shaken severely. Indeed, he stated that he felt the loss so keenly, 'It almost made my faith and principles to totter.'

*   *   *

But though he thus felt his loss, it is evident Jane would not have made him a suitable partner. Even if she had retained her Presbyterian faith, she would not have fitted in as 'a manse wife' and her personality was so strong and her mind so unyielding that there would have been frequent clashing with the equally strong personality in Irving.

As is well known, Jane went on to marry Carlyle and the story of their life together has long been part of the history of English literature.

*   *   *

And Irving and Isabella found a tolerably happy life together.

He was ever the chivalrous gentleman, considerate, patient and kind. And she was a loving and obedient wife. As the daughter of a minister she was able to enter into his activities with a considerable measure of understanding and those of her letters which are extant today show a fine hand and a clear expression of thought. And even the critical Carlyle praised her ability as a housekeeper.

In keeping with Irving's principles they lived frugally. Their door and their table were ever open to the needy, and the only luxuries he allowed himself were his modest wine cellar and his few cigars.

Nevertheless, there can be no doubt he could have benefited from a different kind of wife. Isabella did not possess the wisdom necessary to warn him concerning his tendency to erratic decisions and impulsive behaviour. Had she been a stronger woman much of his later life might have been more balanced than it was and his career might have gone on to the lasting success and triumph which his abilities deserved. It has been well said:

The marriage proved much happier than might have been expected; but it was still the greatest of misfortunes to Irving to have missed a wife capable of advising and controlling him; and found one who could bring him no ballast for the voyage of life.[4]

When Irving entered on the study of prophecy, it turned out to be one for which his rich and surging imagination – never under sufficient control – ill fitted him, while the spell of the mysterious future, believed to be at the very door, laid him open to influences that could but warp his judgment.

DAVID BROWN
Assistant to Irving during 1830–1832,
and later part-author of the Jamieson,
Fausset and Brown *Commentary on
the Old and New Testaments*

9

Babylon and Infidelity Foredoomed

We have seen that under the influence of Coleridge Irving had accepted the idea that mankind was moving, not – as many believed – towards an era of increased blessing, but rather towards a time of universal judgment.

In the mind of students of prophecy this idea seemed remarkably confirmed by the national upheavals of the preceding century.

The first of these was the American War of Independence. The rebellion in 1776 of the Thirteen Colonies and the establishing of a democracy was considered by many an Englishman the work of a spirit of lawlessness and the undermining of the God-given order of government.

But if the English mind was startled by the American revolt it was shocked by the French Revolution. The uprising in 1789 of the oppressed people of France against their rulers – an uprising accompanied by the irresponsible use of the guillotine and the outrages of the Reign of Terror – sent a wave of horror throughout Europe and left many in England in a state of alarm.

The French people discovered, however, they had overthrown a merciless monarch only to bring themselves under a military dictator. This was Napoleon Bonaparte, and from his rise to power in 1795–6 till his final defeat in 1815 he kept Europe almost continually embroiled in war. Moreover, he had about him a certain mysterious force of personality, a power over men of such a nature that many people regarded him as devil-inspired, and numerous Christians were convinced he would eventually prove to be 'the Antichrist'.

But in 1821 Napoleon died and, of course, he had never filled that awesome role. Nevertheless, the dread associated with the name 'Napoleon' did not die with him. He had a son, Napoleon II, and a nephew, Napoleon III, and although they were but youths at this time, there was widespread fear they would grow up to be warlords and possessors of the same mysterious power as their mighty forebear.

Thus the name 'Napoleon' continued to fill people with terror, and this condition, together with the sense of the revolutionary destruction of world order, caused many Christians to believe the world had reached 'the end times', that the Antichrist would soon be revealed, and that the return of the Lord Jesus was very near.

*   *   *

Amid these conditions certain men began to make the coming of Christ their special theme. And particularly prominent in these efforts was a man named Hatley Frere. Frere came of a notable family and his brother had been the British Ambassador to Spain during the Napoleonic Wars. He soon became friendly with Irving, and Mrs. Oliphant says concerning the beginnings of this association:

Mr. Hatley Frere, one of the most sedulous of those prophetical students . . . had propounded a new scheme of interpretation, for which, up to this time, he had been unable to secure the ear of the religious public. . . . Mr. Frere cherished the conviction that if he could but meet some man of candid and open mind, of popularity sufficient to gain a hearing, to whom he could privately explain and open up his system, its success was certain.

When Irving, all ingenuous and ready to be taught, was suddenly brought into contact with him, the student of prophecy identified him by an instant intuition – 'Here is the man!' . . .

He disclosed to his patient hearer all those details to which the public ear declined to listen; and the result was that Mr. Frere gained a disciple and expositor; and that an influence . . . of the most momentous importance . . . took possession of Irving's thoughts.[1]

Frere's new scheme was basically a continuation of the idea Irving had gained from Coleridge – that the world, instead of moving towards a further spreading of the Gospel, was about to enter a period of the greatest suffering.

But whereas Coleridge had based his view on a human assessment of world conditions, Frere based his on an interpretation of two books of the Bible: *Daniel* and the *Revelation*. He asserted that the Biblical prophecies had, at that time, 1824, been almost completely fulfilled and that the coming of Christ could not be more than a few years away.

Irving was indeed, 'all ingenuous and ready to be taught'. He later told Frere that after hearing of his new scheme of interpretation,

I had no rest in my spirit until I waited upon you and offered myself as your pupil, to be instructed in prophecy according to your ideas thereof. . . . I am not willing that anyone should account of me as if I were worthy to have had revealed to me the important truths . . . only the Lord accounted me worthy to receive the faith of these things which He first made known to you. . . .

And if He make me the instrument of conveying that faith to any in His church, that they may make themselves ready for His coming, or to any of the world, that they may take refuge in the ark of His salvation . . . to His name shall all the praise and glory be ascribed. . . .[2]

It is important that we notice the manner in which Irving came into his new views.

In his relations with Coleridge the source of the information was Coleridge's 'high intelligence and great learning' and Irving 'sat at his feet, drinking in every syllable'. And now, in his association with Frere, he simply 'offers himself as his pupil, to be instructed'; 'important truths' are 'revealed' and 'the faith of these things' is 'received'. Frere's views were to Irving a welcome new element of the 'higher style of Christianity' and a valuable area of 'deeper truth' and he accepted them with unquestioning faith.

Thereupon Irving preached a series of sermons on *Daniel* and the *Revelation*, incorporating the ideas he had learned from Frere.

In this work he was in his element. Moved by his vigorous imagination he could immediately fix upon the meaning of 'the beasts', 'the heads' or 'the horns' in *Daniel*, and he had no difficulty in positively identifying the 'two witnesses' in the *Revelation* or determining the significance of every detail of the flight of the woman into the wilderness. His views were stated with dogmatic certainty and the whole was clothed in the ornate splendour of his lofty language.

During recent years there has been a claim made to the effect that Irving was a precise theologian and that his ministry was one of a careful exposition of the Scriptures. This is a kindly gesture towards the good man but it is far from the truth.

One may read through Irving's entire *Works* without finding anything that can truly be termed expository preaching. He takes a text, but uses it merely as a peg on which to hang his own numerous ideas, and the work of the true expositor – the study of the words in the original, and the discovery of the meaning of the text on the basis of those words – is virtually nowhere to be found.

Robert Baxter, a prominent lawyer, who a few years later knew Irving very well, said of him:

His mind is so imaginative as almost to scorn precision of ideas, and his views will thus continuously vary, without himself being aware of it. His energy and activity, swelling into impetuosity, leave him peculiarly open to error, in all subjects which require deep thought and patient and continued investigation.

With the brightest talents, no man was ever perhaps less qualified to investigate and unfold the deeper mysteries of religion, which not only require precision of thought, but a continued watchfulness and patient correction of terms in their statement.[3]

*   *   *

Throughout the next four years – that is, until 1828, at which time he began to take up with the Charismatic teachings – Irving devoted his ministry very largely to the interpretation of prophecy. Undoubtedly, there is much to be said in favour of his action, as he brought a generation which had largely forgotten the reality of the second coming of Christ face to face with its truth. Nevertheless, he constantly went to extremes and was often guilty of 'adding to' the Word of God by making interpretations which came from his own imagination and were in no way founded upon Scriptural statement.

Irving's excursion into prophecy, however, was greatly disliked by many in his Church. This was especially true of the professional and literary people. They considered his speculations utter fanaticism and almost all of this class declared their opposition and ceased to attend his services.

To these people Irving's ministry with its amazing oratory had been little more than a unique form of entertainment. Leaving him they found something else to fascinate them. In the words of Carlyle:

Fashion went her idle way to gaze on Egyptian crocodiles, Iroquois hunters, or whatever else there might be; forgot this man, who unhappily could not in his turn forget. The intoxicating draught had been swallowed; no force of natural health could cast it out.[4]

And William Hazlitt wrote:

Poor Irving is reduced to his primitive congregation; the stream of coronet-coaches no longer rolls down . . . to his Chapel.

They ought never to have done so, or they ought to continue to do so. The world has no right to intoxicate poor human nature with the full tide of popular applause and then to drive it to despair for the want of it.[5]

There can be no doubt Irving had been very proud to have the great ones in his congregation and that he was sorely wounded in losing them.

But he might better have realized he had given them nothing by which their attendance might have been made permanent. They had been drawn to the man and his extraordinary abilities but he had not preached the Gospel to them, the message by which hearts and lives are brought into lowly submission to Jesus Christ and to a lasting desire to be fed upon His Word. The loss of the élite manifested the weakness of Irving's ministry.

Nevertheless, the overall size of Irving's congregations remained as large as ever, for while his emphasis on prophecy drove the great ones away, it also attracted other people, though from lesser walks of life.

*   *   *

Moreover, during his third year in London (1824) Irving came into association with another man who was to exercise a highly important influence in his life. This was Henry Drummond.

Henry Drummond (to be distinguished from a prominent author of the same name in a later generation) came of aristocratic birth and possessed great wealth. Carlyle described him as 'a man of pungent, decisive nature, full of fine qualities . . . but well-nigh cracked by an enormous conceit of himself'. And Irving, upon first meeting him said, 'His words are more witty than spiritual.'

Despite his failings, however, Drummond was truly a good man and Irving soon came to regard him very highly. Drummond was a chief figure in the oversight of a missionary work in Europe, The Continental Society, and notwithstanding the furore caused by Irving's address before the London Missionary Society, Drummond asked him to speak at the Continental Society's 1825 rally.

And again Irving created a furore.

The Society was working in the lands of southern Europe, and

Irving, speaking on the basis of the views learned from Frere, asserted the missionary endeavour had no hope of success. He painted a picture of catastrophic judgment which he declared was about to fall, especially on that part of the world, the old Roman Empire. This, he said, not missionary triumph, lay before mankind.

And again people were highly upset. Several were so angry they walked out while he was speaking and some of the officials of the Society accused him of doing grave harm to their work.

Nevertheless, as on the previous occasion, Irving did not let the matter drop. Rather, he published the address, in a much enlarged form, and entitled it *Babylon and Infidelity Foredoomed*. Babylon was his term for all Christendom, and he declared that because of its infidelity it was doomed, judgment was soon to fall and the coming of Christ was very near.

＊　　　＊　　　＊

These ideas were strongly confirmed for Irving in a book he now came upon: *The Coming of Christ in Glory and Majesty*. This book purported to be written by a converted Jew, Ben Ezra, but the author was actually a Jesuit priest named Lacunza. It was written in Spanish, and in an amazing feat of mental concentration Irving learned the language in a very short time and thereupon he translated and published the book.

The chief feature, however, of the published volume was Irving's 203-page *Preface*. In this he set forth his own prophetic ideas as fully and plainly as in anything he ever produced.

In this present study we are little concerned with Irving's views on prophecy, but our interest relates especially to the development of his beliefs regarding the charismatic gifts. Thus we notice that in the *Preface* he presents the several elements of what he is sure is the Divine programme for the immediate future, one of which he outlines as follows:

When the Lord shall have finished the taking of witness against the Gentiles . . . he will begin to prepare another ark of testimony . . . and to that end will turn his Holy Spirit unto his ancient people, the Jews, and bring them unto those days of refreshing. . . . This outpouring of the Spirit is known in Scripture by 'the latter rain', . . . and like all God's gifts, it will be given to those who will receive it, both Gentiles and Jews. . . .[6]

This is the first mention by Irving of the idea which was later to become all-important in his thinking – that there was soon to come a special 'outpouring of the Spirit', and that this outpouring is prophesied in the Scriptures and is termed 'the latter rain'.

*   *   *

Henry Drummond, moved by Irving's emphasis on prophecy, now made a contribution of his own to the study of the subject.

He announced a Conference to be held at his magnificent country seat, Albury Park, some thirty miles south of London, at which the entire matter of prophecy was to be given intense consideration. The Conference met in November of that year (1826) with some twenty men – ministers and laymen – in attendance and it continued six days.

The view entertained by the Conference was basically that which we have seen enunciated by Frere, but these concepts were discussed with such fervour that the men returned to their homes full of zeal, to cry out to all that 'the end times' had arrived, Antichrist was about to be revealed, and the coming of Christ was very near.

Thus Irving had turned from a more general type of ministry to one which was devoted very largely to the interpretation of prophecy. To him the future was now an open book and in all the enthusiasm of his being he looked forward to seeing the Lord Jesus face to face and he was sure that event, so inexpressibly glorious, was not far distant.

Nevertheless he was equally sure that before that time arrived, God would grant the special 'outpouring of the Holy Spirit', and indeed, that at any moment he might witness the beginning of that outpouring – the 'signs and wonders' of 'the latter rain'.

I well remember when God gave me a son, the most hopeful of his kind, that I devoted him by a solemn covenant unto the Lord from the hour of his birth . . .

And when the Lord cut short his life when it had little more than filled the round of one year, I was stunned and staggered . . . until it pleased Him to reveal for my comfort . . . that the present life, compared to the life of the resurrection, is but like the life of the eaglet in the shell, compared with the life of the mighty eagle who ascends into the height of the heavens and looks into the face of the sun.

IRVING
during the last years of his life

IO

Death Strikes in the Irving Household

During Irving's third year in London his home was blessed with the birth of a son, and he too was given the name 'Edward'. Irving's great heart was moved to this infant with an extraordinary depth of affection. Perhaps his feelings were merely the natural outflow of his exceptionally rich emotional nature, but it is also possible that, since at that time (he had been married but a year) he had not entirely overcome his affection for Jane Welsh, he found a form of release in bestowing so strong a love on his infant son. Carlyle writes:

He had infinite delight in his little baby boy, went dandling it about in his giant arms, tick-ticking to it, laughing and playing to it; would turn seriously round to me, with a face sorrowful rather than otherwise, and say, 'Ah, Carlyle, this little creature has been sent to me to soften my hard heart . . .'[1]

Irving's actions leave us no room to doubt he experienced for this child an affection more intense and more strong than that of the average father.

But all did not go well for the infant. When Isabella was expecting her second child she went to be with her parents in Scotland and, of course, took little Edward with her. The boy was ill and it was thought he would improve more readily in Kirkcaldy than in London.

Two months later Irving joined his family there and to his dismay found that his little boy, instead of getting better, had in fact become worse. Thereupon, day and night he maintained the most earnest prayerfulness, yet, despite his constant intercession, the child's condition deteriorated hour by hour.

Isabella was soon delivered of a healthy baby girl. But while she and Irving looked with rejoicing on the newborn daughter, they watched in helpless sorrow as the life of their infant son ebbed steadily away.

> ... for ten days longer, we are told, in another room in the house, separated from the poor mother, who for her other baby's sake was not permitted ever again in life to behold her first-born, little Edward lingered out the troubled moments, and died slowly in his father's agonized sight.[2]

If Irving's affection for his little son had been extraordinary during his brief life, so also was his sorrow in seeing him taken by death.

Nevertheless, amidst his suffering Irving experienced also a rich measure of Christian consolation. He wrote a letter to William Hamilton, one of his elders in London, and while it contains the tear-filled cry of a broken heart, it also bespeaks a triumphant wiping away of tears and rings with the soul's assurance, 'O death, where is thy sting?'. The letter, written 11 October, 1825, reads:

> Our Dearly Beloved Friend:
> The hand of the Lord hath touched my wife and me, and taken from us our well-beloved child, sweet Edward. . . . But before taking him He gave unto us good comfort of the Holy Ghost . . . and we are comforted, verily we are comforted. . . .
> If you had been here yesterday . . . when our little babe was taken, you would have seen the stroke of death subdued by faith, and the strength of the grave overcome; for the Lord hath made His grace to be known unto us in the inward part. I feel that the Lord hath well done in that He hath afflicted me, and that by His grace I shall be a more faithful minister unto you, and unto all the flock committed to my charge. Now is my heart broken – now is its hardness melted; and my pride is humbled, and my strength is renewed. The good name of the Lord be praised!
> Our little Edward, dear friend, is gone the way of all the earth; and his mother and I are sustained by the Prince and Saviour who hath abolished death and brought life and immortality to light. The affection which you bear to us . . . we desire that you will not spend it in unavailing sorrow . . . and if you feel grief and trouble, oh, turn the edge of it against sin and Satan . . . for it is they who have made us to drink of this bitter cup.
> Communicate this to all our friends . . . and oh, William Hamilton, remember thyself, and tell them all that they are dust, and that their children are as the flowers of the field . . . .
> Your affectionate friend,
> My wife joining with me.
> Edward Irving.[3]

Our hearts go out to Irving and Isabella in their bitter loss.

Nevertheless, the experience, with all its sadness, had its beneficial effects.

Most importantly, it drew the two of them more closely together. After his return to London she remained, recuperating, at Kirkcaldy for some weeks and in many of his letters – he wrote every day – he expresses a new-found and deeper love. For instance, in one such letter he says:

Yea, hath not the Lord made us for one another, and by His providence united us to one another, against many fiery trials and terrible delusions of Satan?

And, as you yourself observed, has He not over again wedded us far more closely than in any joy, by our late tribulation, and the burial of our lovely Edward, our holy first-born, who gave up the ghost in order to make his father and mother one, and expiate the discords and divisions of their souls?[4]

It is possible that in this last sentence Irving is referring to the discord over Jane Welsh, and implying that any lingering affection for her was now crushed beneath the weight of his sorrow.

But the loss of the child brought also a development in Irving's doctrinal beliefs. This was twofold:

One: his statement to William Hamilton, 'it is they [sin and Satan] who have made us to drink of this bitter cup', is the first expression of a view which he held with increasing strength from this time onward – the view that sickness results from sin in the life and that it is in the control of Satan.

Two: he found deep consolation in the fact that little Edward had been christened, and this was the basic concept on which he soon built the further idea that he held the rest of his life – a concept which can barely be differentiated from the doctrine of 'baptismal regeneration'.

Furthermore, Irving emerged from the fires of sorrow a better man. Something of the tendency to self-importance and some measure of the lighter side of his nature was burned away. His pain and suffering did much to offset the harmful effects of his popularity and it was an Edward Irving more suited to serve the Lord who wrote,

Now is my heart broken . . . and my pride melted. . . . I am an unworthy man – a poor miserable servant . . . entirely unworthy to be a minister at the altar of the house of God.

Notwithstanding his unsparing condemnation of evil and worldliness, Irving had so much of the 'celestial light' in his eyes, that he unconsciously assigned to everybody he addressed a standing-ground in some degree equal to his own. The . . . light around him never faded into the light of common day.

Unawares he addressed the ordinary individuals about him as if they, too, were heroes and princes; – charged the astounded yet loyal-hearted preacher, who could but preach and visit, and do the other quiet duties of an ordinary minister, to be at once an apostle, a gentleman, and a scholar; – made poor astonished women in tiny London apartments, feel themselves ladies in the light of his courtesy; – and unconsciously elevated every man he talked with into the ideal man he ought to have been.

MRS. OLIPHANT
Edward Irving, 1864

II

Irving at his Best – and less than his Best

The death of his infant had a lasting effect on Irving. So also did the Albury Conference. The former experience left him a somewhat broken and a humbler man, and the latter, bringing as it did all his prophetic views into concentrated focus, filled him with a new certitude that the end times had arrived and the coming of Christ was very near.

In turn, as a result of having felt the awesome presence of death and of now expecting so soon to see the Saviour, he became in some senses a new man. He manifested a much increased maturity, a strong sense of urgency began to characterize his life and in view of the eternity that lay before him the things of time lost much of their value.

The improved Irving was richly manifested when in March, 1827 –seventeen months after the death of his child and three months after the Albury Conference – he preached at an ordination service. The ordinand was a young fellow-countryman, Hugh Maclean, recently called to the Scots Church, London Wall, where the service was held.

Irving's *Ordination Charge* is characterized by a powerful and passionate intensity which begins with the first sentence and is sustained in unabated strength till the last. In printed form it is undoubtedly the finest production ever to come from his pen, and in its overwhelmingly challenging concept of the ministry we see Edward Irving at his best.

In his opening paragraph Irving commands young Maclean:

... gird up your loins like a man, and hear me while I set forth at length what the Church of Scotland expecteth of your hands in this city. . . . And that I may keep order in my charge, I shall present it to you under these five heads:

– first, the student or scholar; secondly, the preacher or minister; thirdly, the pastor; fourthly, the churchman; and fifthly, the man.

Under the *first* heading he says:

... be instructed ... that the Church expecteth thee to grow in all knowledge and in all wisdom. ... This you must set yourself to do as part of your bounden duty, perfecting yourself in the knowledge of the original tongues, and applying yourself to the critical study of the Scriptures. ...

Besides the careful study of the structure of the Book itself ... I charge you to become acquainted with the history of the Church. ...

And next to this history ... I pray thee, my dear brother, to give all diligence to the study and learning of truth, spiritual or metaphysical, in order that by looking narrowly into the many-sided spirit of man, and its erroneous tendencies to heresy, schism, will-worship and idolatry, thou mayest learn a due caution of thyself, and a right value for the orthodox creed of the Church, which thou must defend against all gainsayers.

... I charge thee, my brother, to arm thyself for the warfare which thou hast to wage against the materialism, the Socinianism, the deism, and the latitudinarianism, which are come up against this city. ...

Make not thyself a mere sermon-maker, or a talker, or a declaimer, or a clerk of religious accounts, or a committee man, or a polite payer of visits, or a drudge of any kind. Seek thy God in thy closet and in thy study; be alone for hours together; be fervent in prayer and meditation; commune with the prophets, and the Apostles, and the saints, and the martyrs, and Jesus, the Author and Finisher of our faith. Do so, I charge thee, that the Church may not be ashamed of thy ignorance or unprofitableness, but rejoice in thee as a good and skilful soldier. ...

Under the *second* heading Irving deals with 'thy capacity as *a minister*' in its relationship to the elements of public worship: (1) the use of Psalms, (2) public prayer, (3) preaching and (4) the sacraments. He declares:

First, then, concerning those Psalms, of which I would not forego one out of the collection for all the paraphrases, hymns and spiritual songs of these Methodistical times. Thou must taste and deeply drink into the spirit of them, and open them to the flock ... for praise without understanding is praise without the heart, not pleasant to the ear of God.

Secondly, thy prayers. ... Oh, it is an onerous charge, my brother, this of public prayer; I cannot tell you how it weighs my spirit down: and I give it in charge to thee to make this part of the ministry thine especial care. Our Church loveth that it should be extempore, and it is best that it should be so; but, oh, fill the fountains of thy spirit every week by secret devotion, and painful meditation, and solemn, careful thought of all things.

Preaching cometh next in order. . . . Here put forth all thy knowledge, all thy wisdom, all thy strength of manhood, with all the gifts and graces of the Divine nature.

Take thy liberty, be fettered by no times, accommodate no man's conveniency, spare no man's prejudice, yield to no man's inclinations, though thou should scatter all thy friends, and rejoice all thine enemies.

Preach the gospel: not the gospel of the last age, or of this age, but the everlasting gospel; not Christ crucified merely, but Christ risen: not Christ risen merely, but Christ present in the Spirit, and Christ to be again present in person.

Dost thou take heed to what I say? Preach thy Lord in humiliation, and thy Lord in exaltation: and not Christ only, but the Father, and the will of the Father. Keep not thy people banqueting, but bring them out to do battle for the glory of God and His Church: to which end thou shalt need to preach them the Holy Ghost, who is the strength of battle. . . .

Lastly come to the sacraments. . . . Give no heed to what is talked upon baptism and the Lord's supper in these clear-headed times. . . . The atmosphere of theology hath been so long clear and cloudless, that there hath not been either mist or rain these many years: and even to talk of a mystery is out-of-date.

NB

But thou must preach Christ in a mystery, and shew the very great mysteries of godliness, especially of these two sacraments. Get thee out of the bright sunshine of the intellect, and meditate the deep mysteries of the Spirit. When they talk of plainness and perspicuity, to thy text, my brother; to thy warfare of prayer and meditation; try the depths, sound with thy deepest line, my brother.

Oh, I charge thee, enter into the mysteries of these two sacraments: if I should hear of thee setting them forth as bare and naked signs, I will be the first to charge thee with a most dangerous error.

Irving's *third* point deals with the minister as *a pastor*.

Of which office, . . . [he asserts], it is the first part to give thy benediction to the flock, to bless them, men, women and children, at thy meetings and at thy partings; not with light words, but with a bishop's blessing.

NB.

Be thou the pastor always; less than the pastor never. Go thus, or go not at all. . . . I will not call thee brother if thou force not thy people to regard thee as their pastor. When thou goest to visit thy people, take an elder with thee. . . . But this in not enough; thy people must come to thee, and seek thy counsel and thy prayers.

Have no idlers about thee: have no spare time. . . . And thou wilt have to lament how few do come to thee for spiritual counsel . . . and how many complain that thou comest not near them in any easy way, to pass an hour and so forth. But go not for any such ends of pastime. But if any say, Remember me in thy prayers, make a note of that, and forget it not; or if he say, Pray for me in such a distress, forget it not. O brother, I know from experience what difficulties abide thee in this field; gird up thy loins and contend with them like a man.

. . . Thou must be willing to give thy life for every one of them, to wash their feet, to minister to them in health or sickness, in wealth and in poverty, in good and in bad report. . . . Feed them, my brother; tend them, my brother; shew forth unto them a shepherd's care. . . .

Fourthly, Irving presents the duty of a minister as *a churchman* – 'an ordained minister of the Kirk of Scotland'. He declares,

Thou art this day one of a body: in the presbytery we expect of thee obedience to the statutes which we obey: in thy session we expect thee to rule and moderate all things according to the laws of the Church. Thou art not thine own master that thou shouldest flinch in anything from that model of church government which God hath blessed to us and to our fathers.

We hinder thee not from brotherly communion with all who are not of the apostasy. . . . But against those who deny Christ's divinity, (these are the true Antichrists,) – against those who have given His glory to another, pope, virgin or saint, (these are the apostasy,) –thou must contend unto the death.

Irving's *fifth* and last point treats of the minister as *a man*'. He gives the warning:

. . . Accumulate riches at thy peril. Oh, if thou grow rich, – oh, if thou shouldst die rich, I will be ashamed of thee. Look at the hard hearts of rich men; look at their vain self-importance; look at their contempt of Christ; and pray, oh earnestly pray, to be kept from that greatest snare.

Thy cloak and thy parchments, brother, – that is, thy decent apparel and thy books, – be these thy riches, and then thou canst speak out against Mammon, and tell those men of thousands and tens of thousands . . . what they should do with their treasures.

. . . Keep thou hospitality. Shew thou to lordly prelates what the word bishop meaneth. Shew thou to substantial citizens what the word hospitality meaneth. Shew thou to rich men what the word charity meaneth; and to all what faith meaneth.

Go thou out as poor a man as thou camest in; and let them bury thee when thou diest. And if God should bless thee with a wife and children, put no money in the bank for them, but write prayers in the record of the book of life; be this thy bank of faith; be this thy exchange, even the providence of

God; and let the lords of thy treasury be the prophets and apostles who went before thee. . . .

Oh, be thou a man far above this world, living by faith in the world to come. . . . Be thou of a bold countenance and of a lion heart, of a single eye and a simple spirit. . . .

If thou art not ready to die, get ready as fast as thou mayest; for the soldier in the battle who is not ready to die hath two enemies to fight: and if thou be not ready to die for Christ, thou mayest have a hundred; but if thou be ready to die for Christ thou hast but one, who is emphatically *the enemy*, against whom, that all thine energies may be collected, give this day all interests, all affections, all gains, all talents, all things unto the Lord, and count them but as dung that you may win Christ. . . .

And now, what sayest thou? Who is sufficient for these things? Thou art, Christ strengthening thee. . . . But what assurance have I, dost thou say? The same which the apostles had, the same which the seventy had, the same which Titus and Timothy and the primitive pastors had, – the Holy Spirit which descended at Pentecost, which hath been present in the Church, which is now present in it, and freely accessible to us all. . . .

I give thee charge in the sight of God, who quickeneth all things; and before Christ Jesus, who before Pontius Pilate witnessed a good confession; that thou keep this commandment without spot, unrebukable until the appearing of our Lord Jesus Christ; which in His times He will shew, 'who is the blessed and only Potentate, the King of kings and Lord of lords; who only hath immortality, dwelling in the light which no man can approach unto . . . to whom be honour and power everlasting. Amen.[1]

Such was Irving's *Ordination Charge*. In its intensity, its fervour and the feeling of urgency which it everywhere conveys it deserves a place alongside Baxter's *Reformed Pastor*, Spurgeon's *Lectures to My Students*, and similar works on the awesome responsibilities of the ministry.

A particular value in Irving's *Charge*, however, lies in the fact that he here reveals something further about himself. The minister he portrays – the thorough scholar, the diligent pastor, the dauntless leader, the man of selfless aims and God-centred desires – is his personal ideal. This is the model he constantly holds before his mind, the man he earnestly seeks that he himself shall be.

And in the making and holding of this ideal we see the true, the essential Irving – Edward Irving at his best.

*   *   *

Nevertheless, like the rest of us, Irving did not always live up to his ideal.

He had matured significantly during his years in London. But his defects were still partially present, and this condition proved painfully evident when, two months after delivering his *Ordination Charge*, he opened his new church.

For some time he had watched with excited anticipation as stone by stone there arose in Regent Square the magnificent new building which was to become the home of his congregation and the centre of his work. It was a grand structure, seating some 1,800, its front adorned by two tall towers patterned after those of York Minster, and the whole of so noble a character as to be worthy of its place as the Scotch National Kirk.

By May of this year (1827) the construction was completed, and in celebration of its opening Irving invited Chalmers to preach at the first service. The church was filled to overflowing for the occasion and, of course, the people had come particularly with a view to hearing the renowned guest preacher.

Here was an opportunity for Irving to practise the principles he had extolled in his *Ordination Charge* – to play a very minor role in the service and to give Chalmers his rightful major part.

But this was too much for Irving. Five years earlier he had left his lowly position as Chalmers' assistant and had come to London with the attitude 'I'll show you what great things I can do!' And now that he had done them – had consistently drawn a congregation of hundreds, had achieved an immense fame and had built this grand edifice – he could not bring himself to fill the secondary role again.

Rather – especially on this prestigious occasion – he must have a prominent part; he must be seen and heard at length, even though by so doing he should disappoint the people and should treat Chalmers with glaring disrespect.

His action is mentioned by Chalmers, who, in writing to his wife, reported:

Mr. Irving conducted the preliminary services in the National Church. There was a prodigious want of tact in the length of his prayers – forty minutes; and altogether it was an hour and a half from the commencement of the service ere I began. . . .[2]

Later in life he mentioned the incident more fully.

Irving at his Best – and less than his Best

I undertook [he wrote] to open Irving's new church in London. The congregation, in their eagerness to obtain seats, had already been assembled three hours. Irving said he would assist by reading a chapter for me. He chose the longest in the Bible [the 119th Psalm] and went on for an hour and a half.[3]

Mrs. Oliphant, though usually highly favourable towards Irving, is critical of his action on this occasion. She declares,

Such an indiscretion was likely to go to the heart of the waiting preacher. Dr. Chalmers seems never to have forgotten that impatient interval, during which he had to sit by silent, and see his friend take the bloom of expectation off the audience, which had come not to hear Irving, but Chalmers.[4]

In Irving's defence it may be stated that he was merely being his usual self. His services were always long – long prayers, long Scripture readings and long sermons, and when his elders repeatedly requested that he shorten the services he was adamant in his assertion that he would take as long as he wished and that *he* was the sole authority in the matter.

Accordingly, in his treatment of Chalmers, as in his regular services, he was simply obeying the stern counsel he had given Maclean:

Take thy liberty, be fettered by no times, accommodate no man's conveniency, spare no man's prejudice ... though thou should scatter all thy friends, and rejoice all thine enemies.

Nevertheless, Irving's thrusting of himself so prominently upon an audience which was waiting to hear Chalmers cannot but be regarded as a display of the old self-importance, much of which had been overcome, but some of which remained. And in this action we see Irving at something less than his best.

Irving's theory of the atonement makes the active obedience and the subjective purification of Christ's human nature, to be the chief features of His work, while the Scriptures make His death and passive bearing of penalty the centre of all, and ever regard Him as one who is personally pure and who vicariously bears the punishment of the guilty.

A. H. STRONG
Systematic Theology, 1886

12

Accused of Heresy – 'Christ's Sinful Flesh'

We have noticed Irving's statement that he had learned more about true Christianity from Coleridge than from all the men he had ever met. And we have also seen that Coleridge did not accept the orthodox belief concerning the Deity of Christ, but he regarded Him as an exceptional human person – a concept well expressed in his words, 'Christ was a Platonic philosopher.'

In turn, shortly after he began to 'sit at Coleridge's feet and drink in every syllable of his conversation', Irving began to preach a view of the person of Christ quite different from that of orthodox Christianity and similar to that of Coleridge. This view he inserted in a somewhat veiled fashion in a series of sermons on *The Doctrine of the Trinity*, and though most of the congregation saw in his statements nothing objectionable, other hearers asserted that throughout these discourses there ran the idea that Christ possessed a sinful nature.

The matter was brought into sharp focus in the following incident.

The Rev. Henry Cole, a Church of England clergyman, attended one of Irving's Sunday evening services. Following the service, shocked by what he had heard, he questioned Irving about his statements, and some days later he published an account of the sermon and the interview. In words addressed directly to Irving he said:

. . . you made me tremble from head to foot by thundering out the expression 'THAT SINFUL SUBSTANCE!' meaning the human body of the adorable Son of God! You were declaring 'that the main part of His victory consisted in His overcoming the sin and corruption of His human nature'. You stated, 'He did *not* sin.' 'But,' you said, 'there was that sinful substance against which

[77]

He had to strive, and with which He had to conflict during the whole of His life upon earth.'[1]

What I felt at hearing such awful blasphemy against the person of the Son of God, declaimed with accompanying vehement gesticulations . . . I cannot describe.

Nevertheless, to put myself beyond the reach of error . . . and at the same time to give you the most fair and full opportunity of unsaying any unguarded expressions, and also to ascertain whether what you uttered was your considerate and real belief, I resolved, if practicable, to speak to you in person . . . and was at length admitted into your presence.

My address and questions, and your answers were as follows: '. . . If I mistake not, you asserted that the human body of Christ was sinful substance?' You replied, 'Yes, I did.' I continued, 'But is that your real and considerate belief?' You answered, 'Yes, it is, as far as I have considered the subject.'

At this point Irving opened a *Confession of Faith* which had been written in Scotland shortly after the Reformation and read out the words, 'The flesh of Jesus Christ, which was by nature mortal and corruptible'.

Upon which I continued, said Cole, 'But do you really maintain, Sir, that the human body of Jesus Christ was sinful, mortal and corruptible?' You replied, 'Yes, certainly. Christ (you continued) did *no* sin; but His human nature was sinful and corrupt; and his striving against these corruptions was the main part of His conflict. Or else (you added), What make you of all those passages in the Psalms, "Mine iniquities have taken hold upon me that I am not able to look up: They are more in number than the hairs of my head, etc., etc.,"? – I answered with astonishment, But surely, Sir, by all those passages are represented the agonies of the blessed Saviour under the number and weight of all His people's sins imputed to and transferred upon Him?.'

'No, no! (you replied) I admit imputation to its fullest extent, but that does not go far enough for me. Paul says "He hath made Him to be sin for us, who knew no sin". . . .'

I observed, 'But if, as you have already allowed, Christ did no sin, how can those passages in the Psalms refer to any sins as being His own sins?' You replied, 'I will tell you what it is and what I mean. Christ could always say with Paul, "Yet not I, but sin that dwelleth in me."'

'What! Do you mean then, (I replied) that Jesus Christ had that "law of sin in His members" of which Paul speaks when he says, "I find another law in my members warring against the law of my mind, and bringing me into captivity to the law of sin in my members"? Not "into captivity" (you replied);

but Christ experienced everything the same as Paul did, except the "captivity".'

'This, Sir,' I observed 'is, to me, a most awful doctrine indeed!'

After twice again asking Irving, 'Is that your deliberate and considerate belief?' and being answered each time in the affirmative, Cole repeated his horror at such a doctrine and therewith closed the interview. A few days later he put his report into print.[1]

Irving declared that Cole's report did not present a true understanding of his doctrine. During the next few years he published scores of pages in an attempt to tell mankind what his view actually was, but in no effort of his whole life did he prove himself so unable to think clearly or to use words precisely. Even the most charitable assessment of his writings in this matter must admit his statements are very hard to understand and that he seems constantly to contradict himself.

Just as in his conversation with Cole he could say in one breath 'Christ did not sin' and in the next could assert 'His iniquities were more than the hairs of his head', so throughout his numerous pages on the nature of Christ he repeatedly makes contradictions of this kind.

It is possible to present a selection of passages from Irving which set forth a certain view of his belief in this matter. But it is equally possible to present a selection of passages which set forth a different view. Nevertheless, after all he said on the subject has been examined, one can find nothing which reveals his belief as plainly as this report from Henry Cole.

*   *   *

But though Irving's doctrine seems strange we must do our best to understand it. It may be summarized as follows:

1. In coming to earth Christ did not take the human nature possessed by Adam *before* the fall, but *after* the fall, and therefore it was fallen, corrupt, depraved human nature.

2. Because of this fallen nature He was subject to the same evil tendencies and the same temptations as other men, and thus His life was a continual battle against sin and Satan.

3. Christ's battle was a real one – as real as that of any man. Irving emphasizes that it would have been unfair for Him to have

had 'God mixed up with His human nature' – such a condition would have given Him an unfair advantage over ordinary human beings. Christ fought our fight – the very battle we all continually experience –subject to all our sinful tendencies and weaknesses.

4. Nevertheless, Christ was always victorious. This, however, was not the result of any special strength in Himself, but it came from the baptism with the Holy Spirit which He received at the beginning of His ministry. The Holy Spirit was so powerfully operative in His life that although His nature was sinful His life remained sinless.

5. Accordingly, Christ is the supreme Example to all mankind. He, in His nature as man, stands before us as the One who always triumphed over sin and Satan. Towards the close of his life Irving published a sermon *Jesus Our Example*[2] in which he urged men to walk in Christ's steps, and this sermon, he said, contained the essence of his view on the Person of Christ and the way of salvation.

6. The Holy Spirit, by whom Christ obtained victory is equally available to all of us, and we may experience the same baptism with the Spirit and be endued with the same power as that which was exercised in Christ.

7. Therefore, Christ, as He came to the close of His activity on earth was able to present to God a perfect human nature. This perfect human nature God accepted, and He did so not merely as to its effect on behalf of Christ, but concerning its effect also on behalf of all mankind. In turn, this acceptance, this coming together of God with man, Irving terms 'reconciliation' and 'at-one-ment' and this great work was accomplished by Christ, not in His death, but in His life.

* * *

Of course, this doctrine propounded by Irving aroused tremendous opposition.

In both England and Scotland men of outstanding ability took up their pens and wrote against the teaching. They asserted, and rightly so, that it made the cross of Christ of none effect – that on such a basis Christ might better have gone directly back to heaven from the upper room without enduring all the sufferings of Calvary.

To these and other such charges Irving replied repeatedly. But in all these efforts to explain and justify his teaching he failed to make anything plain except that he taught 'the sinful substance of Christ' and therefore it was increasingly believed by the public that he looked upon Christ as a sinner.

At this point the author must insert a personal word.

More than once, after spending hours labouring through Irving's *Works* in an earnest effort to understand his belief in this matter, I have put down these volumes with a heavy heart. How sad to realize that so good and sincere and capable a man as Irving was drawn aside from the simplicity of the gospel! Too often he was 'thinking about what is written'. The matter of the Person of Christ is a most profound subject and both the profundity and the limitations of our understanding are well expressed by A. A. Hodge, the American theologian, when he writes:

Jesus of Nazareth was very God, possessing the divine nature and all its essential attributes. He is also true man, his human nature derived by generation from the stock of Adam. These natures continue united in his Person, yet ever remain true divinity and true humanity, unmixed and as to essence unchanged. So that Christ possesses at once in the unity of his Person two spirits with all their essential attributes, a human consciousness, mind, heart and will . . . . Yet it does not become us to attempt to explain the manner in which the two spirits mutually affect each other, or how far they meet in one consciousness, nor how the two wills co-operate in one activity, in the union of one person. Nevertheless, they constitute as thus united one single Person, and the attributes of both natures belong to the one Person.[3]

Irving's error seems to have centred in his separating Christ's human *nature* (which he regarded as fallen human nature) from His Person (which he held to be sinless). He writes: 'When I attribute sinful properties, dispositions, and inclinations to our Lord's human nature, I am speaking of it apart from Him, in itself; I am defining the qualities of that *nature* which He took upon Him, and demonstrating it to be the very same in substance with that which we possess.' He clearly thought that it was possible to ascribe sinfulness to Christ's human nature without implicating Christ's Person.

Irving's teaching had another element which was no less dangerous. This was the way in which he preached Christ's dependence on the power and activity of the Holy Spirit as our example. For instance, some years later he was to say concerning a certain young woman in Scotland:

She came to see what for six or seven years I had been preaching in London, that all the works of Christ were done by the man anointed with the Holy Ghost, and not by God mixing himself up with man. . . . The end of the whole mystery of the incarnation is to show unto mortal men what every one of them, through faith in his name, shall be able to perform . . . .

She straightway argued, If Jesus as a man in my nature thus speaks and performed mighty works by the Holy Ghost which he even promised to me, then ought I in the same nature, by the same Spirit, to do likewise 'the works which he did, and greater works than these'.[4]

On the face of it there is nothing heterodox in such words. But we overcoming sin as Christ overcame sin, we doing the same works as Christ by the Spirit, tended to become the *all-important* element in his teaching. The Christian's foundation, 'Christ died for our sins', was obscured. The substitutionary sufferings of Calvary were not at the centre of his message. It became possible for people to believe that the salvation which Irving preached was salvation by *works* rather than by *grace*.

Why are there no such saints in Scotland now? Because their wine is mingled with water – their food is debased. It will nourish men no longer, but dwarflings.

Oh, Scotland! oh, Scotland! how I groan over thee, thou and thy children, and thy poverty-stricken Church! Thy Humes are thy Knoxes, thy Thompsons are thy Melvilles, thy public dinners are thy sacraments, and the speeches which attend them are the ministrations of their idol.

And the misfortune is that the scale is falling everywhere in proportion, ministers and people, cities and lonely places; so that it is like going into the Shetland Islands, where, though you have the same plants, they are all dwarfed, and the very animals dwarfed, and the men also.

. . . How well the state of our Church, nay, of the Christian Church in general, is described by the account of the Laodicean Church. It almost tempts me to think . . . that these seven Churches are emblems of the seven ages of the Christian Church, to the last of which men are now arrived.

IRVING, 1825

13

Irving at the Height of his Career

Although loud protest was being raised against his doctrine of 'the sinful substance of Christ' Irving made no immediate answer.

He chose first to perform another duty. Having long felt burdened to warn his fellow countrymen of the terrible judgment soon to overtake mankind, he set out on a preaching tour of Scotland. The date was May, 1828, and he was almost thirty-six years old.

The visit was timed so as to make use of a strategic opportunity. The General Assembly of the Church of Scotland was about to hold its annual meetings in Edinburgh, and since almost all the nation's ministers would be in attendance, Irving realized he could reach a large number of them by holding meetings of his own.

Accordingly, upon arriving in the city he announced he would deliver twelve lectures on the *Apocalypse*. But in order not to conflict with the sessions of the Assembly, his meetings would be held at six o'clock in the morning.

The coming of the Assembly always caused a heightened religious concern in Edinburgh, but Irving's presence added a lively excitement. Scots in general were proud of the native son who had achieved such great success in London and now they looked in amazement on his towering dignified figure as he walked the streets, they spoke about his fame as an orator and rejoiced that at last they would be able to hear him for themselves. And no subject could have aroused such fervid interest as the one he had announced, the *Apocalypse*!

*   *   *

Some people may have wondered how many would attend a lecture at so early an hour but they soon had their answer. Irving engaged one of the largest churches in the city, St. Andrew's, and it was immediately overcrowded.

Even Chalmers, on his first attempt, failed to gain entrance.

> Irving is drawing prodigious crowds [he wrote]. We attempted this morning to force our way into St. Andrews Church; but it was all in vain.[1]

Irving then secured another Church, St. Cuthbert's, the city's largest. Yet the overcrowding continued – so much so that two ministers almost came to blows over the accusation that one had attempted to bribe an usher to let him in by a back door.

But Chalmers tried again and this time he arrived early enough to get in. Nevertheless, he was far from happy with what he heard. When Irving had first given evidence of careless statement and strong exaggeration in his interpretation of prophecy, Chalmers had expressed his concern saying, 'I fear his prophecies may unship him altogether', and now, after hearing him lecture, he stated:

> I must just be honest enough and humble enough to acknowledge that I scarcely understood a single word, nor do I comprehend the ground on which he goes in his violent allegorizations, chiefly of the Old Testament.

As an example of Irving's unfounded interpretations we notice the following.

At that time the British Parliament was considering repealing the *Test Act* – a law which made membership in either the Church of England or the Church of Scotland a requirement for the holding of public office. But Irving, strong for the state churches and firm against too free a use of democracy, opposed the repeal. He claimed biblical warrant for his attitude; he asserted that this very repeal was prophesied in the book of Daniel – that Daniel spoke of a fourth Beast who, arising in 'the end times' would 'think to change times and laws' and Irving declared this Beast had now arisen in England and was at work bringing about this repeal. This is the kind of interpretation Chalmers would have considered playing fast and loose with the Word of God.

Chalmers also stated concerning Irving's lectures:

> I have no hesitation in saying it is quite woeful. There is power and richness, and gleams of exquisite beauty, but withal, a mysterious and extreme allegorization, which I am sure, must be pernicious to the general cause.[2]

Nevertheless, the crowds continued throughout the twelve lectures and Mrs. Oliphant remarks:

Whether Chalmers' conclusion was shared by the Edinburgh public seems very doubtful; for to the last, that public, not over-excitable, crowded its streets in the early dawn . . . and his wonderful popularity was higher at the conclusion than at the beginning.[3]

*   *   *

Irving moved on to Glasgow and other communities and everywhere drew large and excited congregations.

But his most important experience took place at Row, a town in the Gare Loch district near the estuary of the River Clyde. He had come to Scotland to instruct others, but here he met two men who instructed him and in so doing altered the course of his life.

The first of these men was McLeod Campbell, the minister of the Kirk at Row.

Campbell had departed to some extent from the teachings of the Church of Scotland. He had rejected the doctrines of human depravity and divine election, and his view of the atonement was that all mankind, though they knew it not, had actually been pardoned through the death of Christ. His message was essentially 'God loves you', and he held that the minister's task lay chiefly in convincing men and women that they were forgiven and teaching them to realize and enjoy the Fatherhood of God. His life was zealous and his preaching warm, and so attractive was his ministry that people came from miles around to hear him. In fact, under his influence the entire Gare Loch area had come into a state of strong religious fervour.

The other man was A. J. Scott, a ministerial probationer who frequently preached for McLeod Campbell and also for Robert Story, minister in the near-by town of Rosneath. Scott was an able man, highly self-opinionated and powerfully persuasive, and Irving spoke of him as 'possessing the strongest faculty for pure theology' he had ever known.

Like Campbell, Scott also had some unusual beliefs. He held the view which we have seen expressed by Irving – that the 'charismata' (the miraculous gifts possessed by the Apostles) had been lost to the Church only because of coldness of heart and a lack of faith. But whereas Irving believed these gifts would be restored during the Millennium, Scott asserted they had never been withdrawn and were still as much available as in the days of Peter and Paul.

Irving was deeply impressed by both Campbell and Scott.

Easily moved, as we have seen, by new ideas – especially if they agreed with his native inclinations – under Campbell's influence he came to reject the doctrines of human depravity and divine election. In place of these he accepted something of Campbell's idea of the Christian message as basically 'God loves you' even though it contradicted his belief that mankind was hastening towards judgment.

And concerning Scott, Irving was so taken with him that he invited him to become his assistant in London. Scott accepted the offer, but did so on the understanding he would be under no doctrinal requirements of any kind.

       *   *   *

Irving preached in the Gare Loch area for some days and his ministry was especially effective.

The religious fervour which already characterized the district had arisen not only from Campbell's ministry, but also from the saintly life of a young woman, Isabella Campbell (no relation to the minister) who had passed away during the preceding year. So important was her influence that we shall give it particular attention later.

Irving's preaching in this area, however, quickened still further the zeal and excitement in the lives of the people. It increased their certainty 'the end times' had arrived and that both the coming of Christ and the administering of divine wrath were very near.

       *   *   *

Before leaving Scotland Irving paid a visit to Kirkcaldy. There a terrible tragedy took place.

On a Sunday evening the congregation which assembled to hear him was so large it dangerously overcrowded the building. Before the service began the galleries suddenly gave way under the excess weight and crashed to the crowded floor beneath. Some people were killed and several were wounded and the panic which ensued caused the wounding of several more.

Irving arrived in the midst of the confusion and standing on a stairway he used his immense strength to lift people through a window and lower them to the ground.

The dead and wounded were carried out and laid in the churchyard. Irving was overcome with sorrow, but as he endeavoured to comfort the suffering a voice arose above their cries, accusing him of being the cause of the tragedy and implying he was heartless about it all.

This accusation, together with his own ideas about the cause of such troubles, wounded him still more. In his belief that sorrow comes as the judgment of God, he was sure the divine wrath was manifested in this tragedy and that it was pointed directly at him. 'God has put me to shame this day before all the people!' he declared, and while we recognize the sincerity of his belief we can but pity him for holding a view so contrary to the Scriptures.

*   *   *

Nevertheless, as Irving concluded his mission to Scotland he could look on it (apart from the tragedy at Kirkcaldy) as a huge success.

Indeed, in this ministry in his homeland his career had reached its peak. It was now six years since his move to London and throughout that time the general direction of his course had been upward. The throngs at the Caledonian Chapel, the eminence of many of his hearers, the circulation of his writings and the construction of the great new Church had been major steps in this progress.

But now, in the triumph of his lectures in Edinburgh, the crowds attracted everywhere else in Scotland, and the acceptance accorded both to himself and his message, his life had touched its zenith and, sad to say, from this point onward his course was to be a downward one.

PART TWO

THE DOWNWARD COURSE

1829–1834

Irving was now preaching in Edinburgh and made a little run over to visit us.

He was very friendly; but he had a look of trouble, of haste, and confused controversy and anxiety; sadly unlike his old good self.... He talked with an undeniable self-consciousness and something which you could not but admit to be religious mannerism; – never quite recovered out of it, in spite of our, especially of her [Jane's] effort, while he staid.

At parting he proposed 'to pray' with us; – and did, in standing posture; ignoring, or consciously defying, our pretty evident reluctance.

'Farewell,' he said, soon after; 'I must go then, – and suffer persecution as my fathers have done!'

THOMAS CARLYLE

14

The Gathering Storm

While Irving had been in Scotland much of the public attitude towards him in England had worsened.

Cole's report had been in circulation for six months and as a result of this and other publications against his doctrine of 'Christ's sinful flesh' the idea that he taught Christ was a sinner was yet more widely believed.

Irving declared this idea was entirely false and that his statements had been misinterpreted.

Accordingly, with the intention of making his view clear he produced a volume, *Six Sermons on the Incarnation*, which he felt would fully answer Cole and all other critics.

But he failed in his intention.

In this book, as in all his writings, there are passages of both beauty and power. Nevertheless, the bulk of it is very difficult to understand, seeming contradictions abound, and nowhere does he provide a simple, straightforward statement of his belief. The book left the idea that he taught Christ was a sinner unexplained and unremoved, and therefore it confirmed that idea in the mind of many.

*　　　*　　　*

Irving found a release, however, from these doctrinal troubles by attending another Prophetic Conference at Henry Drummond's mansion in Albury.

The Conference met in December of this year (1828) and the chief outcome was the decision to publish a Quarterly Journal of Prophecy. This took the name *The Morning Watch* and, aided by Drummond's extensive financial support, it was a high-quality production – the finest of printing on the best of paper, together with excellent editorship.

The Conference was also given a piece of information which was considered particularly important. Irving reported it in Drummond's words:

. . . that the [ten lost Hebrew] tribes have been discovered, twenty millions in number, inhabiting the region north of Cashmere and towards Bohara, in the great central plain of Asia. It would seem that there came men from them to Leipsig fair . . . they were trading in Cashmere shawls.[1]

The news of this discovery was looked upon by the Conference as further evidence 'the end times' had arrived. (A short while later, however, it was declared by one of Irving's followers, that the American Indians were the ten lost tribes and that they all would soon emigrate to Palestine.)

*   *   *

As 1829 progressed Irving laid plans to make another trip to Scotland.

He intended that this mission would duplicate that of 1828 – he would again be in Edinburgh while the General Assembly was in session and again he would hold a series of meetings of his own. There can be no doubt but that he hoped to repeat the previous year's success.

But he soon found the attitude towards him had changed.

First, his letters to one minister after another requesting a church in which to meet were answered by refusals. As a result he determined to preach out-of-doors and ordered the printing of several large placards, each carrying the announcement of his lectures and stating that his subject would again be the Apocalypse.

Let these be stuck up [he said to a friend in Edinburgh] on the corner of every street. . . . I believe the Lord will not fail me in this purpose, from which nothing on earth shall divert me. I will do it, though they should carry me bound hand and foot to prison.[2]

Secondly, Irving planned that this time he would be a participant in the Assembly, and not, as before, merely a spectator. Thus, on his way to Edinburgh he stopped at Annan and had himself commissioned as representative of the Borough of Annan at the Assembly.

Upon reaching Edinburgh he presented his plan. But the Assembly considered it nothing more than personal propaganda and totally rejected it.

Moreover, no one was willing to allow him the use of a church. The only place available was a small suburban chapel, and here he delivered his early morning lectures.

It gave me no pain at all, he wrote, to be cast out of the Assembly. . . . My lectures are decidedly producing an impression upon the people. The work of the Lord is prospering in my hand. . . . The Commissioner [the King's personal representative to the Church of Scotland] asked me to dine with him. . . . I enjoyed myself vastly with the Solicitor General and Sir Walter Scott. . . .

It is hard work standing forth, with an extempore sermon of two hours, every morning at seven o'clock. . . . The number of ministers attending is very remarkable.[3]

Irving moved on to Glasgow and there he met both reception and rejection. His old friends, the Calton weavers, welcomed him most heartily. But several in the congregation at St. John's were disrespectful under his preaching and as he left the Church some who stood around manifested their strong dislike.

'Ye're an awful man,' cried one. 'They say you preach a Roman Catholic baptism and a Mohammedan heeven.'[4]

Better things, however, awaited him elsewhere. He visited several towns, preaching at times in churches but more often in fields, and his congregations sometimes were numbered in the thousands. There was virtually no opposition and he was received, as formerly, as 'a man sent from God.'

And again he visited the Gare Loch area. And this time also his ministry stirred the already intensely fervent people, increasing the hope they had gained from A. J. Scott that the charismatic gifts would be restored, and assuring them of the soon coming of the Saviour.

Yet, despite the reception accorded him in the latter part of his journey, it was plain to Irving that the general attitude towards him in Scotland was vastly different from what it had been the year before and that to many of his fellow countrymen he was now *persona non grata*.

* * *

When Irving returned to London he found himself at the centre of a literary warfare.

Several authors, among them two or three men of high capability, had written against what they termed 'the Heretical Doctrine of the Reverend Edward Irving'. Newspapers editorialized on the matter and Irving's doctrine was made the subject of many a sermon.

But Henry Drummond and others replied on Irving's behalf. And Irving himself came into the fray. His style was frequently belligerent. Above all, he still did not state his doctrine plainly, and people continued to believe he spoke of Christ as a sinner.

And month by month this battle was maintained.

*　　　*　　　*

In 1830, however, opposition from the Presbyterian ecclesiastical authority began to appear.

It was directed first against Irving's friends, McLeod Campbell, Hugh Maclean and A. J. Scott. Each was cited to appear before the next session of the General Assembly to answer concerning charges of heresy. We shall notice the outcome later.

But denominational opposition was raised against Irving too.

After some preliminary skirmishing during the Spring and Summer, Irving was ordered to stand trial before the London Presbytery in October. The charge was heresy concerning his doctrine of 'the sinful substance of Christ'. The Presbytery was composed of merely three ministers and three elders, and these men had it in their power – or so it seemed – to dismiss him from the ministry.

There was, however, a technicality involved. The Trust Deed of Irving's Church stated that its minister must be ordained by a Presbytery in Scotland. Irving interpreted this requirement as freeing him from any relationship to the London Presbytery. Therefore after the trial opened he informed his would-be judges that he was not obliged to submit to their petty adjudication and in high dignity he walked out of their Court.

The Presbytery, of course, continued the trial. It heard the evidence against him and found him 'guilty of heresy' on four counts, as charged.

Thereupon the Elders and Deacons of Irving's Church took action on his behalf. They published a statement in which they declared their personal adherence to the great truths of the Christian faith, including specifically the assertion that the Lord Jesus was 'very God and very man, yet one Christ'. And they asserted this was what Irving had always believed and preached.

Such an assertion, however, indicates they had failed to understand what he had actually been preaching. It reveals that, like many other hearers, they had been fascinated by his oratory, but had failed to grasp the true nature of his teaching.

*   *   *

But though Irving had delivered himself temporarily from the authority of the London Presbytery, he could not fail to see that the tide of public opinion had turned strongly against him. His friends Campbell, McLean and Scott were soon to stand trial before the General Assembly and it was evident it would not be long before he too would meet the same fate.

Nevertheless, in the midst of such circumstances, Irving was unmoved and unmovable. He was convinced he was fighting for the truth and that his opposers were the ones guilty of heresy. With all his being he believed Christ was kept from sin by the Holy Spirit and that therein lay the very essence of Christianity – that mankind, too, may have the same measure of the Spirit's power, and experience the same victory.

The preaching of Mr. Campbell of Row, which had stirred the whole countryside . . .; the proceedings against him then going on before the ecclesiastical courts . . . ; the repeated apparition of Irving, – then perhaps the most striking individual figure in his generation, and who spread excitement . . . around him wherever he went, – had combined to raise to a very high degree of fervour and vividness the religious feeling of that district.

Several humble persons in the locality had become illustrious over its whole extent by the singular piety of their lives, piety of an ecstatic, absorbing kind. . . . Religion was not only the inspiration of their hearts, but the subject of their thoughts, discussions and conversations.

MRS. OLIPHANT
The Life of Edward Irving

15

'The gift of tongues' in Scotland

In the chapter which reported Irving's visit to the Gare Loch area of Scotland in 1828, mention was made of a young woman, Isabella Campbell.

Some two or three years earlier Isabella had become ill with tuberculosis. Thereafter she was frequently confined to her sick room and as the months passed she meditated much on the things of God. At times her sense of the Divine presence was so real she seemed almost unconscious of things around her. 'Whether in the body or out of the body' she hardly knew and in these experiences her countenance became radiant and her speech flowed forth at length in a spontaneous ecstasy of communion with God.

In 1827, at the age of twenty, Isabella passed away.

Shortly thereafter her minister, Robert Story, wrote an account of her life. He entitled it *Peace in Believing*, and so beloved was her memory that within weeks nearly every home in the entire area possessed a copy. The book had no particular literary merit but it well portrayed her saintly character and reported especially her ecstatic experiences.

The account of Isabella's life had two effects.

One: it moved people to seek this kind of high religious feeling in their own lives and thus it made the ecstatic experience the great *desideratum* throughout the already intensely aroused district.

Two: it caused numerous people to visit the Campbell home. The Campbells were a fatherless family living on a small farm at Fernicarry. After Isabella's death there remained two sons and two daughters, and the home was maintained by the struggling labours of the widowed mother.

The visitors came to the Campbell home to honour Isabella's memory, and their attitude was virtually that of pilgrims visiting a shrine.

Needing, however, something more tangible than the memory of a departed one on which to bestow their veneration, they turned to Isabella's younger sister, Mary. Therewith there began for this girl – then in her late teens – a career which brought her into wide prominence, particularly in the charismatic movement which was soon to develop.

We must familiarize ourselves with this extraordinary young woman.

A young man whom Mary had expected to marry had recently passed away. She was heart-broken – so much so that her health had suffered and although she continued to make her living as a dressmaker, she was at times quite ill. Her ailment, however, was different from that of Isabella – it was

... not ordinary tubercular consumption, but the formation of large abcesses on the lungs, which from time to time burst, and in doing so reduced the patient to extreme weakness. During the intervals she would rally and enjoy comparatively good health.[1]

Her minister describes her, saying:

She was a woman of great personal attractions, had a beautiful face, and soft eyes, with drooping lids, which she seldom raised. She was very clever, and, considering her obscure circumstances, was well informed.

Her character, however, lacked the moral strength of Isabella's, and her enthusiastic mind was not so strictly controlled as might have been desired. . . . There was in her, in fact, much of the nature and disposition which have, from age to age, furnished the Church with mystics.[2]

Story also remarks on the adulation bestowed on Mary by the visitors to the Campbell home. He states:

A young, beautiful, not highly educated, and withal excitable invalid, could not but suffer a certain distortion of the *morale* of her nature, and be led – insensibly, it may be – towards the borders of delusion and vanity, when she found herself the cynosure of the eyes of a large portion of the religious public, and beheld some company of its pilgrims ever and anon resorting to her shrine.

Among those who thus came to Fernicarry, were some whose minds were much engaged with the idea to which, at the time, Mr. Irving's teaching had directed public attention, *viz.*, that bodily disease was the direct infliction of Satan, and that therefore faith and prayer, and these only, should be employed as the means of deliverance from it; and that, moreover, by the due exercise of these, the power of effecting miracles of healing and other wonderful works would be restored to the Church. . . .

The subject of missions was also profusely talked about in Mary's sick room, and the idea of a due preparation for evangelistic work was more or less bound up with the new notions regarding the restoration of spiritual gifts. To Mary herself, the central point in all the discussions . . . that went on around her, was the preaching of the Gospel to the heathen. A small band of intended missionaries gathered at Fernicarry – funds were collected – clothes provided – and prayer was made to God continually that their way might be directed according to His will.[3]

Moreover, evening by evening this band of intended missionaries gathered in Mary's room. The noise of their talking, singing and praying severely disturbed her brother, Samuel, who also was sick and, in fact, was near death in the room below. Two of these young men had of their own accord taken residence in the Campbell home and when Mr. Story spoke to them about thus eating the bread of poor Mrs. Campbell they answered him, 'Get thee behind me, Satan!'

These youths then went on to tell Story God had called them to become missionaries and that therefore He had directed them to live at the Campbell home. Story asked why they were not learning the language of the people to whom they hoped to minister, and was told, 'No preparations of that kind were needful; and unbelief alone could suggest such carnal preliminaries.'

*　　　*　　　*

In the midst of these circumstances Mary became subject also to the strong influences of A. J. Scott.

It will be recalled that Irving, at the close of his first mission to Scotland (1828) had taken Scott to London to serve as his assistant. Irving had long believed that the supernatural gifts the Church had possessed in Apostolic times would be restored, but he assumed this restoration would not take place till the beginning of the Millennium. But from Scott he learned otherwise. He wrote:

. . . as we went out and in together, he used often to signify to me his conviction that the spiritual gifts ought still to be exercised in the Church; that we are at liberty, and indeed bound, to pray for them, as being baptized into the assurance of 'the gift of the Holy Ghost' as well as of 'repentance and remission of sins'.

... Though I could make no answer to this, and it is altogether unanswerable, I continued still very little moved to seek myself, or to stir up my people to seek these spiritual treasures. Yet I went forward to contend and to instruct whenever the subject came before me in my public ministrations . . . that the Holy Ghost ought to be manifested among us all, the same as ever He was in any one of the primitive Churches.[4]

During his days as assistant to Irving, Scott paid another visit to the Gare Loch area of Scotland. Again he preached in the pulpits of Row and Rosneath and again he visited people in their homes.

One person to whom he gave particular attention was Mary Campbell. Irving says:

He was led to open his mind to some of the godly people in these parts, and among others, to a young woman who was at that time lying ill of a consumption, from which afterwards, when brought to the very door of death, she was raised up instantaneously by the mighty hand of God.

Being a woman of a very fixed and constant spirit, he was not able, with all his power of statement and argument, which is unequalled by that of any man I have ever met with, to convince her of the distinction between regeneration and the baptism with the Holy Ghost; and when he could not prevail he left her with a solemn charge to read over the Acts of the Apostles with that distinction in her mind, and to beware how she rashly rejected what he believed to be the truth of God.[5]

Scott's words proved of historic significance. His making a 'distinction between regeneration and the baptism with the Holy Ghost' was the first mention anywhere in the Irvingite movement of the two-stage concept of the Christian life – a concept that soon became highly important.

And Scott's 'solemn charge' proved effective.

In a letter to her minister, written a few weeks later, Mary spoke as from the standpoint of this second stage – of having come into a new and superior relation to the Holy Spirit. This is evident in her opening words:

My dear Mr. Story, – I have not been at liberty to attempt writing to you until this present moment. I bless God who does not suffer me NOW to write when *I* please, but WHEN *He* pleases and WHAT *He* pleases. There is NOW to me a delightful depth of meaning in the words being BIDDEN and FORBIDDEN by the Holy Ghost. . . .[6]

Throughout the letter she talks of matters being directly revealed to her by the Holy Spirit and she sees the miraculous working of the Spirit in minor details – in things in which a miracle was in no way necessary. For instance, one morning it was impressed on her mind that she would that day receive a letter from a certain person and during the day the letter arrived, and she considered her early premonition supernatural. Her letter to Story is long, and throughout it her thought is turned inward in a mystical introspectiveness, with attention constantly being given to the state of her emotions and the effect of her impressions.

But over and above her new relationship with the Holy Spirit, Mary was expecting something much more. She looked forward to receiving two of the Apostolic gifts: the first 'the gift of tongues' and the second 'the gift of prophecy'.

These gifts were bound up in her thinking with the intended foreign missionary enterprise. 'We possess,' she declared, 'the character of those upon whom the Lord hath promised to pour out in the last days His Spirit, and "they shall prophesy".' The other young people who composed the group of intended missionaries looked to her for advice, and concerning her counsel to one of them she stated:

I could not urge him to commence the study of languages, seeing I look every day for the gift of tongues, &c., being poured out upon the Church. I am sure nothing hinders these things but the infidelity of His own children.

I look upon the system of education for the ministry to be of the Devil. . . . If God has promised to furnish His servants with every necessary qualification for their great work, what have they to do but step into the field, depending on *Him* for *all?* . . .

But there is another consideration that prevents me from saying to anyone to study, in order to qualify himself for the work of the Lord. And it is this – *the time is short*. I expect to see the Redeemer on earth long before one . . . could be ready or fit, according to the judgment of men, for entering into the field of Christian labour.[7]

Thus Mary Campbell's circumstances were extraordinary, and we must notice them again:

One: the area in which she lived was alive with religious fervour and the faith of the people was the strong, unquestioning kind. *Two:* Irving's visits had raised the feelings of the people still further concerning the soon coming of the Lord Jesus: 'time is short'. *Three:* the strongly persuasive A. J. Scott had convinced Mary that regeneration may be followed by 'baptism with the Holy Ghost' and that the Apostolic gifts, particularly those of prophecy, healing and tongues, are still just as available as they were in New Testament times. *Four:* she was assured that sickness was of the Devil, but could be overcome by faith. *Five:* she intended to become a missionary and was convinced that no language study was necessary but that all requirements would be met supernaturally.

Moreover, this girl, uneducated but natively brilliant, had suddenly come out of obscurity into a blaze of popularity. People from many parts of Scotland visited her in her home and made her the object of admiring attention. She was surrounded by a group of young people (one of them a young man whom she was soon to marry) who were fascinated with her ecstatic experiences and who constantly prayed for her healing.

But above all, both Mary and this company around her had one supreme expectation in mind – she was to be the first to experience the renewed outpouring of the charismatic gifts – she was to receive 'the gift of tongues'. And in high anticipation they awaited the moment of its arrival.

Nor were they disappointed – indeed, their deep longings were soon fulfilled.

Irving, who was in London at the time, wrote an elaborate account of the event, speaking of Mary as experiencing a 'seizure of the Holy Ghost'. But Robert Story who was near by and spoke from personal knowledge, reported as follows:

On a Sunday evening in the month of March [1830], Mary, in the presence of a few friends, began to utter sounds to them incomprehensible, and believed by her to be a tongue such as of old might have been spoken on the day of Pentecost, or among the Christians of Corinth.[8]

This was, of course, an historic event. It was the first experience of 'speaking in tongues' in the Irvingite movement.

Moreover, Mary was sure she was not merely uttering incomprehensible sounds. She was certain she was speaking a language – she asserted it was the language of a people on a remote island in the South Seas – the Pelew Islanders – a people of whom she had been reading.

And to this gift she shortly added another: that of automatic writing.

At times she would pass into a kind of trance-like condition in which she would seize a pencil and with amazing speed fill pages of paper with script. The characters she used were not those of the English nor any other known language and therefore the whole experience was believed to be miraculous and the writing was said to be in a foreign tongue.

News of Mary Campbell's 'gift of tongues' spread rapidly. It soon reached much of Scotland and many parts of England. And among the people of the Gare Loch area, already so highly aroused, it came as undeniable evidence of the presence and power of God, confirming their faith and increasing their fervent excitement.

*　　　*　　　*

Moreover, others in Scotland were also to receive the gift.

A few miles down the Loch, in the town of Port Glasgow, there lived a family named McDonald. This family, friends of the Campbells, was composed of two brothers, James and George (each thirty years of age) and three sisters, Jane, Mary and Margaret, the last-named in her late teens.

Like most people in the area the McDonalds had come under the teaching about the gifts. This was first through the preaching of McLeod Campbell and, indeed, the brothers had earlier placed their sisters in lodgings at Row for some months in order that they might sit under his ministry. To this there had been added the strong persuasions of A. J. Scott and finally the powerful influence of Irving in his two preaching missions throughout the area.

The McDonalds were quiet people, intensely earnest in Bible reading and prayer, and, like Mary Campbell, were highly introspective, much concerned about their feelings, and about impressions and revelations.

Margaret McDonald was also a semi-invalid. Early in 1830 she had an experience in which she received, she said, 'the gift of prophecy'. And a little later (three weeks after Mary Campbell's 'tongues' experience) the two MacDonald brothers had a similar experience and each 'spoke in tongues'.

In the midst of these events James McDonald was moved to seek healing for his ailing sister. She was not bedridden, but lay much of the time on a couch. James took his stand alongside her, and grasping her by the hand commanded, 'I say unto thee, arise!' Margaret made no move, whereupon James repeated the command and this time she rose to her feet and shortly after declared herself 'healed'.

James immediately wrote a letter to Mary Campbell. In it he reported Margaret's experience and commanded her likewise to 'Arise!'

The next morning James went down to the dock to await the arrival of the ferry which carried passengers from the upper part of the Loch. And when it arrived, whom should he see but Mary Campbell! Upon reading his letter she too had arisen from her couch, and now, 'healed', she had come to tell him what had happened!

The minister at Row, McLeod Campbell, learning of these events, paid a visit to the McDonald home that he might see and hear for himself. He hoped the tongues were of divine origin, but in order to test them he said they ought to be interpreted. Thereupon James broke out into incomprehensible sounds and George gave an interpretation, 'Behold He cometh – Jesus cometh.'

*　　　*　　　*

Thus, in the space of one month, during the early part of 1830, in the Gare Loch area of Scotland, experiences had taken place which were claimed to be 'the gift of tongues', 'the gift of prophecy', 'miraculous healing' and 'the interpretation of tongues'.

Certain facts about these phenomena must have our special attention.

One: 'the gift of tongues' did not come as an unexpected and sudden outpouring from heaven. Rather, it was something which was looked for and it came gradually, as the oft-experienced ecstatic speech gave way to incomprehensible sounds.

Two: these phenomena did not arise, as some have claimed, amidst a ministry of thorough expository preaching and doctrinal teaching. Instead, the ministry of McLeod Campbell was notable chiefly for its fervour, that of A. J. Scott for its emphasis on the gifts and that of Irving for its stress on the soon return of the Lord Jesus.

Three: the condition of the people was not one of strong biblical learning, but rather of high religious emotion.

Nevertheless, thus there had begun what were claimed to be the Apostolic gifts, the phenomena which were henceforth to command Irving's attention, to remould his activity – indeed, to govern his activity throughout the rest of his days on earth.

*　　　*　　　*

'The gift of tongues' in Scotland

Following her experience, Mary and her friends continued to meet upstairs in the Campbell home as usual, praying especially that all of them might receive 'the gift of tongues' and thus be equipped to begin their missionary careers.

But in the room beneath there still lay Mary's brother Samuel and he was now near to death. Moreover, he was 'racked through his whole frame by the shouting and leaping and singing overhead'. Yet despite his condition 'he rallied . . . his decaying energies, left his pillow and ascended the stairs . . . entered the room and entreated them to be quiet'. But, like Pastor Story, the dying man was told (not by Mary but by some of her companions), 'Get the behind me, Satan!'⁹ And in a few days' time he had passed away.

Mary and her friends, however, were not prepared to accept this as the end. Their prayers for Samuel's healing had not been answered, but now, claiming Christ's promise 'Greater things than these shall ye do', they gathered round the corpse praying for the greater miracle – that of resurrection – a request which resulted in disappointment.

*   *   *

But Mary did not long remain at home.

Conditions there were backward and Fernicarry was a place of little importance. Thus, before a few months had passed she moved to Helensburgh, the most populous town in the area and there she proved a still greater centre of attraction. Robert Story speaks of her 'in the midst of those tumultuous meetings in Helensburgh . . . receiving the homage of all classes of these religionists who were panting after novelties'¹⁰ as she told of her own experience and also helped to bring others into the experiencing of 'tongues'. Moreover, by this time she claimed that besides the language of the Pelew Islanders she now could speak Turkish and Chinese.

Despite her activity at Helensburgh, however, Mary had her eye on greater things and before long she moved to where they were possible – the Irving Church in London and the Drummond mansion in Albury.

The character of the sound has perhaps received as many different descriptions as there are persons who have heard it.

To some the ecstatic exclamations, with their rolling syllables and mighty voice, were imposing and awful; to others it was merely gibberish shouted from stentorian lungs; to others an uneasy wonder, which it was a relief to find passing into English, even though the height and strain of sound was undiminished.

MRS. OLIPHANT
The Life of Edward Irving

16

'The gift of tongues' in London

News of the phenomenal happenings in Scotland spread swiftly to London.

All manner of explanations as to their origin were given. Some people said they were the result of deception on the part of the participants, others asserted they were merely psychic in nature, and still others attributed them to Satan.

But Irving had no doubt in the matter. He was convinced they came from God and that they marked the beginning of the colossal event that A. J. Scott had declared was to be expected – the restoration of the Apostolic gifts.

'I did rejoice with great joy,' he stated, 'when the tidings were read to me . . . that the bridal attire and jewels of the Church had been found again.'[1]

And in this joy he prayed with increased fervour that these gifts might now be outpoured upon London too.

*   *   *

Irving regarded his own circumstances at this time, however, as indicating the hand of the Lord was upon him, not in any such blessing, but rather in judgment.

That is, his fourth child, Samuel, a babe a year old, was ill and, in fact, seemed near to death.

Irving viewed this as something more than just the sickness of a beloved infant. We have seen his belief 'that bodily disease is the direct infliction of Satan, and that therefore faith and prayer, and these only, should be employed as the means of deliverance from it'.

But despite this belief, two physicians had been called in. It appears, however, that Irving had been away from home at the time and it is possible that Isabella alone had taken this action. At any rate, upon learning what had been done, and considering it an affront to the Lord, Irving endeavoured to make the best of the situation by combining the two methods – that is, by having the doctors not only perform their professional labours but also by having them pray. Thus, in a letter to Isabella he stated his desire that the doctors should

. . . do for the dear babe whatever they can, and do it in faith as far as they are enabled; joining the prayer of faith to their use of means.

Withal, my confidence is with the chief Physician, and I feel only the more trust, as I see the case to be the more extreme. . . . My dear, we must not treat Christ as a common physician, or believe that He has not remedies because the physicans have none. May the Holy Spirit grant us strong and lively faith for our dear child![2]

Hereby Irving maintained his principle and at the same time gently pointed out to Isabella the error of resorting to medical aid.

Yet notwithstanding the faithful intercession of the parents and probably of the doctors too, the little life slowly weakened and before long passed away. And Irving could not but have found his sorrow deepened by his belief, first, that sickness and death are in the control of Satan and, secondly, that in seeking the help of the doctors they had gone against the plan of God.

*   *   *

Moreover, the suffering was undoubtedly increased for Irving and Isabella by the contrast between their case and that of a Miss Fancourt who, at this very time, experienced what was considered miraculous healing.

Miss Fancourt, a young woman of well-to-do circumstances, had been in a semi-invalid condition for some months. Having no need to be active she had adopted an attitude of weakness and said of her frailty, 'It is sent in mercy.' This acceptance of illness seems to have been her outlook since girlhood and her ailment was manifestly merely functional and not something organic.[3]

A young man of her acquaintance, however, declared with strong assurance that Jesus could heal her. Then, with much kind, yet firm, suggestion, he convinced her she was able to arise and walk and under the strength of his influence she did so. During the days which followed, under the steadily positive attitude, the muscles, long partially used, regained their strength, till her walking, though still somewhat feeble, seemed almost normal.

Miss Fancourt's 'healing' immediately received wide attention. Because of the publicity already given to the experiences of Margaret McDonald and Mary Campbell this case also caught the public fancy and was accepted by many as a clear instance of miraculous healing. And to Irving Miss Fancourt's experience was of paramount importance. He saw it as evidence that the restoration of the Apostolic gifts was not to be limited to Scotland. Here, indeed, was the first sign it was to be granted in England too, and though he sorrowed over the death of his child he rejoiced in the Fancourt 'miracle'.

*   *   *

The news of the Gare Loch events aroused such interest that a party of Londoners set out to visit the area that they might examine the phenomena for themselves. The date was September, 1830 – some five months after Mary Campbell's initial experience. The party, all of whom appear to have been members of the Church of England, was headed by a lawyer, J. B. Cardale, and with him were his wife and sister, a physician named Thompson and two other men. They visited the Campbell home and the McDonald home and heard people speak in tongues, and after spending three weeks in the area they returned to London to report their findings.

In presenting his report before a number of interested persons Cardale stated that after careful consideration he was convinced the gifts were supernatural. He also declared that the people involved were above any suspicion of deception and he emphasized his certainty that the tongues were not mere unintelligible sounds, but were actual languages. Cardale affirmed:

The voices were in connection with each other, euphonious; many of them were evidently inflected, and they conveyed the impression of being well-formed and cadenced languages.

The persons, while uttering the unknown sounds, as also while speaking in the Spirit in their own language, have every appearance of being under supernatural direction.[4]

These opinions, coming from the lawyer Cardale and the physician Thompson – men whose training fitted them to make a knowledgable judgment in such a matter – carried much weight. In the mind of many, Cardale's report removed all doubt as to the genuineness of the gifts and, as a result, the two assurances, (1) that the work was supernatural and (2) that the tongues were languages, became the settled belief of a majority among the interested persons in London.

*   *   *

These assurances awakened a still stronger desire to see the gifts outpoured upon London too.

Several people opened their homes for prayer with the definite purpose of claiming the promise 'I will pour out my Spirit upon *all* flesh'. These meetings, characterized by intense earnestness and strong expectancy, were carried on throughout the autumn and winter of 1830–1831.

And then, in the spring, the answer came!

In April, Mrs. Cardale 'spoke in tongues'. With great solemnity she uttered three phrases in incoherent sounds. She also interpreted what she said, declaring her unknown words meant. 'The Lord will speak to His people! The Lord hasteneth His coming! The Lord cometh!'

Nor was this all. A few days later, Miss Hall, a young woman who attended Irving's services, both spoke in tongues and sang in tongues.

We must try to realize the excitement that would be aroused by these events. In the mind of many they were entirely supernatural, a direct display of the mighty power of God and the first instance in England of the restoration of the long-lost Charismata. Here was the answer to the months of praying. The delight of many knew no bounds.

*   *   *

Irving, however, though he joined fully in this rejoicing, again found it necessary to turn his attention to other matters.

The General Assembly of the Church of Scotland was to meet in Edinburgh in May and, as we have seen, his friends, McLeod Campbell, A. J. Scott and Hugh Maclean, were then to be placed on trial, charged with heresy. In view of this situation Irving had already inaugurated a special prayer meeting in his Church. It met at 6.30 in the morning and despite the hour it was remarkably well attended.

The Assembly met and did its work and for Irving and his people the verdict was a sorry one. Campbell was deposed from the ministry, Scott was deprived of his licence to preach and McLean was ordered to appear before his local Presbytery that it might deal with him as it should see fit.

Moreover, the Assembly's action did not end there. It was also directed against Irving. The Assembly decreed that if he should ever again attempt to preach on Scottish soil, the Presbytery in which he thus appeared should place him on trial concerning his doctrine of 'the sinful substance of Christ'.

*   *   *

Nevertheless, any hurt which Irving felt by this treatment at the hands of men was much lessened for him by what he deemed the blessing of God. The tongues were now being experienced with increased frequency and he reported:

> We cried unto the Lord for apostles, prophets, evangelists, pastors and teachers, anointed with the Holy Ghost, the gift of Jesus, because we saw it written in God's Word that these are the appointed ordinances for the edifying of the body of Jesus. . . .
>
> The Lord was not long in hearing and answering our prayers. He sealed first one, and then another, and then another, and then another; and gave them first enlargement of spirit in their own devotions, when their souls were lifted up to God and they closed with Him in nearness; He then lifted them up to pray in a tongue . . . the Spirit took them and made them speak in a tongue, sometimes singing in a tongue, sometimes speaking words in a tongue; and by degrees, according as they sought more and more unto God, this gift was perfected, until they were moved to speak in a tongue even in the presence of others. . . .
>
> Then, in process of time, perhaps at the end of a fortnight, the gift perfected itself, so that they were made to speak in a tongue and to prophesy; that is, to set forth in English words for exhortation, for edification and comfort. . . .[5]

What Irving thus says about the 'gift of tongues' must be noticed.

(1) In London, as in Scotland, the ability to speak in tongues was preceded by a highly aroused condition – that which he terms being 'lifted up to God and with Him in nearness' – a condition similar to

the ecstasies of Mary Campbell. (2) It did not appear suddenly, nor come upon the subject in completed form. Rather, it came gradually and a period of time elapsed before it became fully operative. (3) The unintelligible sounds were usually followed by words in English; these were considered the 'interpretation' and the two activities together were termed 'prophesying'.

Accordingly in Irving's own statements there is much to suggest the tongues were largely an induced and cultivated skill – a suggestion which, as we shall see, received strong confirmation from other sources.

*   *   *

This work went on throughout the summer months of the year we are considering (1831) and, as a result, by the beginning of September a considerable number of persons in Irving's Church were able to 'speak in tongues'.

Moreover, a handful among this company had attained a particular importance. Four of these were women: Mrs. Cardale; her sister-in-law, Miss Emily Cardale; Miss Hall and Mary Campbell. Two were men: Edward Taplin and Robert Baxter. These six were known as 'the gifted ones', and they sat together in a prominent pew during the Church services.

It must be pointed out that these were not poor and unlearned people. Rather, with the exception of Mary Campbell, they were well-to-do and were associated with professional walks of life.

Mrs. and Miss Cardale were respectively the wife and the sister of a successful lawyer.

Miss Hall was the governess in the home of Spencer Perceval, a man who was a Member of Parliament and whose father had been England's Prime Minister.

Edward Taplin was a teacher who operated his own Academy and was well versed in languages.

Robert Baxter was the senior partner in a prominent law firm.

Mary Campbell, as we have seen, though she had received but small education, possessed a very capable mind and a certain mystical genius. She had recently been married; her husband was a young law clerk named W. R. Caird and the two of them still talked of becoming missionaries.

These six composed a kind of inner circle around Irving. Because

1. *A pencil sketch of Irving, drawn by Joseph Slater, c. 1825.*

2. *A view of Haddington, Scotland, where Irving worked as a school-teacher after leaving Edinburgh University.*

3. *Thomas Chalmers, whose assistant Irving became in 1819 at the age of twenty-seven.*

4. *The Caledonian Chapel, Hatton Garden, London, Irving's first church.*

5. *The pulpit of the Caledonian Chapel.*

6. The exterior of the new building, the National Scotch Church, later known as Regent Square Church. When the Caledonian Chapel proved too small, Irving's congregation moved to this new building in 1824.

7. *The interior of the National Scotch Church.*

8. *The Albury Park Conference of 1826. This reconstruction of the first prophetic conference of the nineteenth century drawn by H. Anderson, shows Henry Drummond, the owner of Albury, addressing Hugh M'Neile at the head of the table. Irving is facing Drummond and on his right is David Wilson, later Bishop of India.*

9. *A wax relief of Irving by an unknown artist.*

10. *A water colour of Irving, by an unknown artist, c. 1823.*

of their facility in speaking in tongues and interpreting they were considered 'prophets' and they were held in high esteem by those in the church who favoured the gifts.

*　　　*　　　*

Much of the strength of this charismatic activity arose from the fact that the tongues were widely believed to be actual languages.

We recall Mary Campbell's certainty in this regard. She could not urge missionary candidates 'to study languages, seeing I look every day for the gift of tongues. . . . What have they to do but step into the field, depending on *Him* for *all?*' She went on to state, 'The time is short', and the idea held by herself, by Irving and many others was that the ability to speak a foreign language without having learned it, was the means whereby Christianity's message would be carried throughout the world in the short time remaining before the return of Christ.

This was not a new idea. Rather, for centuries it had been believed that the gift of tongues, instead of being the production of unintelligible sounds, was the ability to speak a language which had not been learned. This had been the claim of the Montanists in the second century, and of the several groups which used 'tongues' during the Middle Ages. The biographers of such Roman Catholic missionaries as Francis Xavier and Vincent Ferrer made it appear these men spoke in unlearned languages, although such claims did not stand up under examination. 'Tongues' appeared also among the persecuted Protestants of France in the seventeenth century and there were reports of these people – even children – who knew nothing but their own patois, speaking in Latin and Greek.

Moreover, at the very time in which the 'tongues' appeared in Scotland and London, similar things were taking place in America. The Mormons, who took their rise in 1830, underwent experiences of the same nature as those of the Irvingite movement. The Mormons spoke in unintelligible sounds, and this they claimed was 'the gift of tongues'. And they declared they were able by this means to speak the language of the Indians nearest them, but that the gift would be enlarged, first to include all the Indian tribes of the continent and later all the nations of the world.

Likewise, the Shakers in America professed the same gift and one of their leaders – a woman – claimed she possessed 'the gift of tongues' in more than seventy languages.

And Irving, in his native bent towards the mystical, was not only highly fascinated by the tongues, but also had no doubt they were actual languages. He reports:

The whole utterance from the beginning to the ending of it, is with a power, and strength, and fulness, and sometimes rapidity of voice, altogether different from that of the person's ordinary utterance . . . and I would say, both in its form and in its effects upon a simple mind, quite supernatural. There is a power in the voice to thrill the heart and overawe the spirit . . . . There is a march, and a majesty, and a sustained grandeur in the voice, especially of those who prophesy, which I have never heard even a resemblance to. . . .

It is a mere abandonment of all truth to call it screaming or crying. . . . And when the speech utters itself in the way of a psalm or spiritual song, it is the likest to some of the most simple and ancient chants in the cathedral service. . . .

Most frequently the silence is broken by utterance in a tongue, and this continues for a longer or a shorter period. . . . So far from being unmeaning gibberish, as the thoughtless and heedless sons of Belial have said, it is regularly-formed. well-proportioned, deeply-felt discourse, which evidently wanteth *only the ear of him whose native tongue it is*, to make it a very masterpiece of powerful speech.[6]

Thus Irving, like others, was sure that to speak in a tongue was to speak a foreign language.

*   *   *

But Irving's own condition, amid this outpouring of gifts, was strange. Though he was the leader in the whole development he had received no charismatic gift of any kind.

The reason, however, may not be hard to find.

It is evident Irving did not want any gift which needed some form of human inducement. The gift of tongues did not come as a direct action from heaven, but means were usually employed to bring it about. Miss Cardale was considered especially proficient in this regard and made it her practice to say to a seeker, 'Yield your tongue, yield your tongue, yield your tongue to the Holy Ghost!' Likewise, Mary Caird, with her mystical but forceful personality, did much instructing as to how to speak in tongues and was exceptionally successful in the task.

Irving condoned these practices, but he wanted something better for himself. He dare not accept any form of the gifts which might leave him with the least doubt as to the supernaturalism of the phenomena – he must have an experience so clearly miraculous that it would constantly confirm his faith and strengthen his conviction that the whole activity was of God.

And he looked for just such an experience.

He anticipated the coming on him of 'the power' in what he spoke of as 'a mighty seizure of the Holy Ghost' – an experience in which he would receive not only the gift of tongues, but the 'baptism with fire', and the power to perform all manner of miracles. In keeping, he believed, with the promise in the closing verses of Mark's Gospel, he asserted that the restoration of the charismatic gifts would include the power to handle serpents and consume poisons without hurt. The experience which he expected would be of such a nature as to be unquestionably Divine and, although God had not yet granted it, with all his heart he believed it was coming, and with great longing he awaited its arrival.

Nevertheless, although Irving bore up well in the face of his difficulties, the nervous strain was telling upon him physically. The abounding vigour and vitality he had always enjoyed was fast leaving him and, though he was yet but thirty-nine, we are told he now '. . . looked hollow and haggard, thin, grey-whiskered, almost an old man'.

The McDonalds [of Port Glasgow] *never could be prevailed upon to acknowledge the claims and doings of their brethren in London. They could not but 'mourn for their very great blindness'. They solemnly warned them of the danger they were in 'from erroneous views of the work of the Spirit', 'giving the lordship to the Spirit and not to Christ'.*

EDWARD MILLER
The History and Doctrines of Irvingism,
London, 1878

17

The Gifts in Action

Among the many persons drawn to Irving's work by an interest in the tongues, a chief figure was a former Deist named George Pilkington.

Pilkington began to attend the early prayer meetings and before long, in one of these gatherings, he found himself 'strongly excited by a very powerful feeling'. He restrained himself from speaking, but a few days later he felt a power so strong it could not be held back and he burst forth, making such statements as 'Deny me no more!' and 'The second sword is now drawn in this church'.

Though he spoke in English and not in a tongue, Irving was much impressed. Pilkington reported:

Mr. Irving praised God for 'opening another mouth', and said, 'We have heard the voice of the shepherd.' I now concluded that the excitement I felt was the same as that which influenced 'the gifted persons', but that they experienced it in a higher degree, which produced the utterance of a tongue.[1]

Pilkington immediately went on to seek the gift of tongues, but his concept of the phenomenon was different from that of other people. Since he was a man of considerable learning and had a knowledge of several languages, he did what was natural to him – he tried to translate the words spoken in tongues into English.

He provides examples of this endeavour.

Hearing a woman utter the sounds *gthis dil emma sumo*, he stated they meant ' I will assume this dilemma'. Another woman's utterance sounded like *Hozequin alta stare, Hozehamenanostra*, and this he translated as 'Jesus in the highest will take care of this house'. A third woman's utterance, *Casa sera hastha caro*, he said was Spanish and that it meant 'The house will be in my care'. *Yeo cogo nomo* was for him 'I know the law', but he dismissed the utterance *Holimoth holif awthaw* as merely 'Holy, most holy father' in poorly enunciated English.

Pilkington felt his efforts were a help to Irving's cause. He was sure the tongues were in three languages, Latin, Spanish and Italian, and he believed that in showing them to be not unintelligible sounds, but actual languages, he was proving them to be truly supernatural.

The tongues people, however, were of a different mind. They looked with strong dislike on his translating and this was especially the attitude of Robert Baxter. Baxter told him that in these efforts he was not acting 'in the power' but was labouring solely 'under the excitement of the flesh' and that his translations were made by 'the human understanding'. He was told this use of the understanding was a terrible error and that the meaning of a tongue – a miraculous utterance – could only be known by an equally miraculous occurrence – an interpretation given by the Holy Ghost.

Pilkington was sorely disturbed: first, at having his interpretation rejected in this way and, secondly, in finding himself linked with a movement in which, in order to maintain its beliefs, he was required to inhibit his understanding. Therewith doubts as to the genuineness of the whole charismatic concept began to arise in his mind. But he endeavoured to subdue them, desiring in no way to oppose Irving, 'whose persuasive eloquence and transcendent ability were so attractive and irresistible'.

Nevertheless, his doubts continued, and indeed increased.

For instance, Irving had designated two periods during the prayer meeting at which he allowed the tongues to be spoken. But Pilkington noticed the speakers could bring on 'the power' at the first permitted moment and could likewise shut it off the moment the period ended, He remarked

. . . how instantaneously they burst forth as if the trigger of a loaded gun had been pulled, when Mr. Irving declared the law permitted them to speak in the Spirit . . . and how suitably they could restrain the Spirit till the second service . . . apparently with as much ease as . . . a stop watch.[2]

Pilkington asked questions about these things but he received no satisfactory answers. He was told he must not seek natural explanations of supernatural events and that in attempting to understand Divine activity human intelligence must be put aside.

Such excuses, however, only increased his doubts, and as the weeks passed, despite his love for Irving, he more and more lost faith in the gifts. Finally he decided he could continue his relationship with an activity of this kind no longer. He met with Irving, had a friendly discussion, but bade him farewell and therewith left the movement.

Some weeks later, feeling that a knowledge of his experiences would be a warning to others he published a pamphlet:

THE UNKNOWN TONGUES
Discovered to be English, Spanish and Latin
and the
Reverend Edward Irving
Proved Erroneous In Attributing These Utterances
To the Influence Of

THE HOLY SPIRIT

Various interesting colloquies between the writer and Mr. Irving and his followers, and observations which manifestly show they are all under a delusion.

By

GEORGE PILKINGTON

Who Interpreted Before The Congregation

The publication of this pamphlet with its accusation of 'delusion' was a sore blow for Irving.

*   *   *

The tongues practices, however, increased in both frequency and fervour. And of course there were strong differences of opinion as to their origin and nature.

To many people it was unquestionable that they were supernatural. Such people shared with Irving the belief that the tongue speech was inspired and therefore for them the whole practice was overshadowed with a sense of the miraculous. Moreover, many persons who spoke in tongues testified that the experience brought them new joy and strength in their daily lives.

But there were also numerous others who believed the tongues were of a merely human origination.

For instance, the Rev. Hugh McNeile, a Church of England clergyman who had officiated as Moderator at the Albury Conferences, at first endeavoured to view the activity as miraculous. But he was soon forced to change his mind. McNeile's attitude was represented in his statement about hearing Taplin, the school teacher, speak in tongues:

I write in all seriousness before God, without scoff or sneer or ridicule, but simply a *bona fide* description of what I heard. It was neither more nor less than is commonly called jargon, uttered *ore rotundo* and mingled with Latin words, among which I heard more than once *amamini, amaminor*.[3]

Some observers, however, were less gracious in their remarks. One said of his visit to an Irving meeting:

I could not see the speaker, or to be more correct, the roarer. I should judge by its harshness that it was the voice of a man. It lasted but a minute or two and ran off into English words, 'Abide in Him! Ye shall behold His glory! Ye shall behold His glory.'

The whole was uttered in a tone of varied cadence, but so loud, revolting and unnatural (not unearthly) that it operated on me like a shock from which I could not immediately recover. . . .

The speakers at Irving's seem to lose all self-control and to be operated on by a foreign influence.[4]

There were also eye-witness accounts which contained such statements as: 'the terrific Crash (cras- cras- cra- Crash!!!) with which the utterance began': 'a violent exertion of the muscles at the back of the jawbone': 'She screamed on till, from exhaustion, her voice gradually died away': 'Suddenly an appalling shriek seemed to rend the roof, which was repeated with heart-chilling effect . . . and then suddenly a torrent of unintelligible words. The young lady was quite scarlet.'

And Thomas Carlyle left a report of an experience in this regard. Speaking of himself and Jane he says:

. . . going next evening to call on Irving, we found the house all decked out for this same 'speaking with tongues'; and as we talked a moment with Irving who had come down to us, there rose a shriek in the upper story of the house, and presently he exclaimed, 'There is one prophesying, come up and hear her!'

We hesitated to go, but he forced us up into a back room, and we could hear the wretched creature raving like one possessed; *hooing* and *haaing* and talking as insensibly as one would do with a pint of brandy in his stomach, till after some ten minutes she seemed to grow tired and became silent.

Nothing so shocking and unspeakably deplorable was it ever my lot to hear. Poor Jane was on the verge of fainting and did not recover the whole night.[5]

Several further statements of a similar nature could be cited but the above are sufficient to show the attitude of many who came into contact with the tongues.

*   *   *

By now, however (September, 1831), Irving's Church had become divided over the charismatic practices.

One faction was composed of the staid Presbyterian members – men and women whose concept of a Sabbath service was one of reverent worship of God and to whom any disturbance was abhorrent.

The other was composed of persons who had been drawn either by Irving's prophetical speculations or by the tongues, and to most of these people the solemnities of worship meant little and the 'manifestations' meant much.

Between these two groups there had been strong differences of feeling since the tongues first began.

Nevertheless, Irving had been able thus far to prevent a clash. Despite the clamouring of the tongues people that they be allowed to speak in tongues during the church services, he had permitted the practice only in the early morning prayer meeting, and forbade it in the church.

But it was evident this condition could not long continue. Those who wanted the tongues were strong in their demands and week by week their insistence increased.

Moreover, Irving was going against his own convictions and he knew that sooner or later he must remove all controls and permit those who possessed the gift to use it whenever they desired.

His attitude is manifest in a letter he now wrote to his father-in-law, Dr. Martin. It reads:

26th October 1831

My Dear Father:

Thanks should be returned in all the churches for the work the Lord has done and is doing amongst us. He has raised up the order of prophets amongst us, who, being filled with the Holy Ghost, do speak with tongues and prophesy.

I have no doubt of this; and I believe that if the ministers of the Church will be faithful to preach the truth, as the Lord hath enabled me to be, God will seal it in like manner with the baptism of the Holy Ghost. . . .

I desire you to rejoice exceedingly, although it may be the means, if God prevent not, of creating great confusion in the bosom of my dear flock. For as prophesying is for the edification of the Church, the Holy Ghost will require that His voice shall be heard when 'the brethren are come together into one place'; and this, I fear, will not be endured by many. But the Lord's will be done. I must forsake all for Him, I live by faith daily, for I daily look for His appearing.

Your dutiful and affectionate son,

Edwd. Irving[6]

And Irving's fears of 'great confusion within the bosom of his dear flock' soon proved true. The tongues, almost forcibly, made themselves heard in the church – a development which came about in the following manner.

On a Sunday morning, Miss Hall, as she sat in the congregation, found she could not restrain an utterance which welled up within her. She arose and rushed to the vestry, trying to muffle the sounds as she ran. In the vestry she continued the utterance and finally the words 'How dare ye to suppress the voice of the Lord?' burst forth from her lips in a tone loud enough to be heard in the church.

But while Miss Hall was in the vestry another woman was moved to utterance, and rising from her seat she 'ran down the side aisle and out of the church through the principal door'. An eye-witness reported Miss Hall's action, saying:

The sudden, doleful and unintelligible sounds, being heard by all the congregation, produced the utmost confusion; the act of standing up, the exertion to hear, see and understand, by each and every one of perhaps 1500 or 2000 persons, created a noise which may be easily conceived.

Mr. Irving begged for attention, and when order was restored, he explained the occurrence, which he said was not new, except in the congregation, where he had been for some time considering the propriety of introducing it; but though satisfied of the correctness of such a measure, he was afraid of dispersing the flock; nevertheless, as it was now brought forward by God's will, he felt it his duty to submit.[7]

When the service was over, Irving, together with his elders and deacons, met with Miss Hall. She was in no way apologetic for what she had done, but rather, with all the authority of a prophet, she told Irving that out of servile fear of offending the Presbyterians he was restraining the Spirit of God. And she boldly reminded him that 'Jesus hid not His face from shame and spitting, and that His servants must be content to follow Him without the camp, bearing His reproach'.

To such a man as Irving the accusation of being unwilling to suffer for the sake of Christ could not but come as a thrust to the very heart. Upon hearing her charge he was quite overcome, fell back on a chair and 'groaned aloud in distress'.

During the afternoon, news of the morning's events spread rapidly and brought together an immense congregation at the evening service. Mrs. Irving's sister (the wife of William Hamilton, one of the elders) reported:

... there was a tremendous crowd. The galleries were fearfully full; and from the commencement of the service there was an evident uproariousness ... men's voices continually mingling with the singing and the praying in most indecent confusion.

Mr. Irving had nearly finished his discourse, when another of the ladies spoke. The people heard for a few minutes with quietness comparatively.

But on a sudden a number of the fellows in the gallery began to hiss, and then some cried 'Silence!' and some one thing and some another, until the congregation, except such as had firm faith in God, were in a state of extreme commotion. Some of these fellows (who ... it afterwards appeared were a gang of pickpockets come to make a *row*) shut the gallery doors, which I think was providential – for had anyone rushed and fallen, many lives might have been lost. ...

Mr. Irving ... immediately rose and said, 'Let us pray', which he did, using chiefly the words, 'Oh, Lord, still the tumult of the people'. This kept those in the pews in peace, none attempted to move, and certainly the Lord did still the people.

We then sang, and before pronouncing the blessing, Mr. Irving intimated that henceforth there would be morning service on the Sunday, when those persons would exercise their gifts, for that he would not subject the congregation to a repetition of the scene they had witnessed. ...

A party still attempted to keep possession of the church. One man close to me attempted to speak. Some called 'Hear! Hear!' others 'Down! Down!' It was very difficult to get the people to go, but by God's blessing it was accomplished.[8]

*   *   *

Of course Irving was greatly upset by this disgraceful disturbance.

Nevertheless, he refused to let it move him from his conviction that the tongues must be permitted in the services. Thus on the following Sunday,

He stated that if it pleased the Lord to speak by His messengers, he begged [the people] to listen to them with devout attention.

In a few seconds a female (we believe, Miss Cardale) comenced in the unknown tongue, and then passed into the known tongue. She said, 'He shall reveal it! He shall reveal it! Yea, heed it! Yea, heed it! Ye are yet in the wilderness. Despise not His word! Despise not His word! Not one jot or tittle shall pass away.'

The minister then rose and called upon the church to bless the Lord for His voice which they had just heard in the midst of the congregation.[9]

Thereafter, Sunday by Sunday, the voices of the tongues speakers sounded forth in the services. Irving still tried to exercise control: he designated two periods in the service, one early and one later, during which this activity might take place, but these limits were seldom observed. Sometimes the voices were orderly, but often they were not, and the sudden shriek, the painful groan and the incoherent harangue sounded forth in many a Sabbath service.

Understandably, the Presbyterian people with their love of reverence were outraged by the allowing of such proceedings in the house of the Lord. Some left the Church, but others, moved by their admiration for Irving, remained and fondly hoped for the best.

Nevertheless, it was evident to the members of both factions that the division was deep and that a direct confrontation, with all its attendant harm, could not long be avoided.

One man, however, stood out above all others, in his advocacy of the charismatic gifts and in carrying his practices to extremes: this was Robert Baxter.

The prevalent belief of the Church has been, that in the Pentecostal gift the disciples received a supernatural knowledge of all such languages as they needed for their work as Evangelists. The knowledge was permanent and could be used at their own will, as though it had been acquired in the common order of things. With this they went forth to preach to the nations. . . .

Augustine thought that each disciple spoke in all languages; Chrysostom that each had a special language assigned to him, and that this was the indication of the country which he was called to evangelize. Some thought that the number of languages spoken was 70 or 75, after the number of the sons of Noah, or the sons of Jacob, or 120 after that of the disciples. Most were agreed in seeing in the Pentecostal gift the antithesis to the confusion of tongues at Babel, the witness of restored unity.

E. H. PLUMPTRE article, 'Tongues, Gift of' in
Smith's Dictionary of the Bible

18

Robert Baxter and 'The Baptism with Fire'

We have seen Robert Baxter as one of 'the gifted ones' in London, but now must make his acquaintance more fully.

Baxter's home and law practice were at Doncaster in the north of England, yet his professional duties frequently brought him to London – possibly for weeks or months at a time.

He was an earnest member of the Church of England, and was active in Sunday School teaching and in efforts to help the poor. But he prayed to see a true reviving of God's work and when he heard of the phenomenal happenings in Scotland, followed by those in London, he was thrilled and longed that he might experience such things himself.

Accordingly, when next he went to London he immediately attended Irving's early morning prayer meeting. At that date (August, 1831) the tongues were not yet allowed in the Church service, but they constantly occurred in the prayer gathering. Baxter attended this meeting, and did so, not with any thought of examining the phenomenon, but, he says, with his mind already made up and 'fully convinced the power was of God'.

And he was not disappointed with what he found. Of this first meeting he reports:

After one or two brethren had read and prayed, Mr. Taplin was made to speak two or three words very distinctly, and with an energy and depth of tone which seemed to me extraordinary, and it fell upon me as a supernatural utterance, which I ascribed to the power of God; the words in a tongue I did not understand.

In a few minutes Miss Emily Cardale broke out in an utterance in English, which, as to matter and manner and the influence it had upon me, I at once bowed to as the utterance of the Spirit of God.

Those who have heard the powerful and commanding utterance need no description; but they who have not may conceive what an unnatural and unaccustomed tone of voice, an intense and rivetting power of expression – with the declaration of a cutting rebuke to all who were present . . . would effect upon me . . . .

In the midst of the feeling of awe and reverence which this produced, I was myself seized upon by the power; and in much struggling against it, was made to cry out . . . after, to utter a prophecy that the messengers of the Lord should go forth, publishing to the ends of the earth in the mighty power of God the testimony of the near coming of the Lord Jesus.

I was overwhelmed by this occurrence. The attainment of the gift of prophecy, which this supernatural utterance was deemed to be, was, with myself and many others, a great object of desire. . . .

There was in me, at the time of the utterance, very great excitement; and yet I was distinctly conscious of power acting upon me beyond the mere power of excitement.[1]

Thus upon his first attendance at an Irving meeting Baxter received 'the gift of prophecy'. This was regarded as a gift which included the 'baptism with the Holy Ghost' and was accounted superior to the baptism itself.

In turn, since he was thus conspicuously favoured of God and was a man of earnest Christian activity as well as professional standing, he was considered a valuable addition to Irving's work and was immediately accorded a place among 'the gifted ones'.

* * *

This experience marked a point of basic alteration in Baxter's life.

He shortly returned to Doncaster and as the weeks passed it was evident he was a changed man. His spiritual life was improved, as with increased earnestness he prayed and fasted and with new boldness he witnessed for Christ. Likewise his joy was new and he frequently experienced times of ecstasy, saying for instance of one such occasion, '. . . my soul was filled with joy and thanksgiving, and with such a presence of God as exceeded any peace and joy I had ever tasted'.

Baxter read his Bible, but not in any thorough or consecutive study. Rather it was to him something like a collection of mottoes, and he could find in a verse here or a verse there a confirmation of some preconceived idea, or could fix upon the action reported in some Bible narrative and could regard it as a Divine directive for his own life.

Occasionally Baxter spoke in tongues. This, however, he considered an experience of little value. He took it for granted the tongues were actual languages, but since none of the native people who used them were available he regarded the gift as useless, except in the case of missionaries going to a foreign land.

For Baxter, the much superior experience was that of being 'in the power'.

This was for him a very definite condition. He was aware of the precise moment 'the power' came upon him and equally aware of the moment it left.

He believed 'the power' was solely the work of the Holy Spirit. He says it came on him 'accompanied with the flashing in of convictions upon the mind, like the lightning rooting itself in the earth', and these flashings he regarded as revelations from heaven, giving him infallible directions as to actions he must take and granting to the words he spoke while 'in the power' the quality of divine inspiration.

Moreover, 'the power' was something over which he had no control. Of one experience he says, '. . . the utterance was so loud that I put my handkerchief to my mouth to stop the sound, that I might not alarm the house'. And on another occasion, while he was teaching in Sunday School 'the power' came upon him so mightily that he could not continue the teaching, but was forced to hasten to his home, there to receive from the Holy Spirit distinct directions concerning activities to be undertaken the following day.

Thus Baxter's life became virtually governed by 'the power'.

The attitude he developed was one of almost constant introspection, an unrelenting concern about impulses and impressions. His convictions, coming as they did, 'like lightning rooting itself in the earth', proved so strong they frequently overruled the dictates of common sense. The trained legal mind ceased much of its normal functioning and his life came largely under the control of something as mystical and uncertain as the comings and goings of 'the power'.

Baxter also was constantly looking for miracles. The ordinary workings of natural law lost much of their meaning for him and he interpreted any events which were not easily explainable, and many that were, as miraculous.

Under these circumstances Baxter's moods were far from steady. He was often puzzled about Divine directions and his periods of joy sometimes gave way to confusion, and the maintaining of his feeling of euphoria became a main endeavour of his life.

*   *   *

Baxter's forwardness in the exercise of 'the power' was manifested when next he returned to London.

While conducting a meeting a few days after his arrival, he offered to answer, speaking 'in the power', any questions which might be put to him.

He gave several replies but one seemed especially miraculous –in reporting a certain event he mentioned several details of which he could not possibly have been aware by natural means. They were matters entirely beyond his knowledge and many of his hearers were overawed, believing he could have spoken such things only by Divine revelation. The occurrence was declared an unquestionable miracle and was considered an evidence that he had received still another of the charismatic gifts, 'the gift of knowledge'.

*   *   *

Baxter also undertook to preach. Of one of these efforts he reported:

Here again the power was most abundant upon me; and I was, for the space of near two hours, made to give forth to them what was called by the Spirit 'preaching in the Spirit', a sermon setting forth the course of the church since the Apostles' days.[2]

The sermon likened the church to Samson, shorn of his strength, and it emphasized that the strength was now returning – the Apostolic gifts were being restored.

But the sermon contained also one extraordinary pronouncement:

. . . count the days, one thousand three score and two hundred – 1260 – the days appointed for a testimony, at the end of which the saints of the Lord should go up to meet the Lord in the air. . . .[3]

It was 14 January, 1832, when Baxter made this statement, and therefore he was setting the date of the coming of Christ as 27 June, 1835. He also repeated the statement on several occasions during the next few months and it became accepted by Irving and many others, if not as the exact date, at least as an approximate one. Thus from this time forth the majority in the Irvingite movement believed the return of Christ would probably take place not later than 1835 or 1836.

* * *

In his practice of acting upon impressions received while 'in the power', Baxter more than once did something incredibly extreme.

For example, he tells of an occasion on which he was 'overwhelmed' with the certainty that God was commanding him to bear an extraordinary witness for Him before the High Court of Chancery.[4] He was to enter the Court and cry out to the Lord Chancellor in denunciation of 'the darkness of the Church of England', and he was to accuse the Chancellor, as 'keeper of the conscience of the King' with personal responsibility in the matter. He realized he would therewith lose his professional status and would probably be cast into prison, but these things he was willing to bear for the sake of obeying God.

He immediately acted to carry out the command.

Though suffering tremendously in his inner self he entered the Court. He took up a suitable position and then stood waiting for the power to come upon him, ready, as soon as it arrived, to make his fearful denunciation.

But an hour went by, and another hour, yet all the while he felt no power. He continued to wait, two more hours passed and still he felt nothing. Embarrassed by the failure he told himself he might have misunderstood the Divine directions, and then in utter confusion and deep despair he walked out of the Court.

* * *

Nevertheless, a few days later he received another revelation and this was even more startling. It ordered him to leave his wife and family and become a wanderer upon the face of the earth – this as a judgment upon his wife for her refusal to believe in the charismatic manifestations.

This time, however, he was given a sign assuring him these directions would not – like those of the Court affair – prove erroneous. The sign was that he was to visit his brother, Ashley Baxter, a clergyman living in the east of England, and that upon arriving,

I should find my brother at home; and as I entered his paddock gate, he would come out of the house to meet me – that whilst I was there he should receive the Spirit and speak in the same power with which I spoke.

That . . . I should be made in power to deliver to him two messages: one to be carried by him to my wife, to declare to her what God's purpose concerning her was, and the other to be borne to some relations, enjoining upon them the winding up of all my worldly concerns, and the future provision for my wife and family.

That a child of my brother should also be called as a prophetess, and that I should minister on the ensuing Sunday in my brother's church – that when my brother went to carry the message, he should also be commissioned to baptize with the Holy Ghost my youngest child, an infant of six weeks old.

I was in great trouble upon this revelation. The conclusion I gathered from it was that I should never see my wife again.[5]

When he arrived at his brother's home matters fell out just as he had envisioned.

As he entered the paddock gate Ashley came out to meet him and shortly thereafter received the Holy Spirit and spoke in the power. The next day Ashley left for Doncaster and on the ensuing Sunday Baxter preached in his brother's church. He says that Ashley's wife, 'under the nervous excitement was seized with an hysteric fit,' but he also states that several hearers were mightily blessed by his ministry.

When Baxter returned to London he was to meet opposition from unexpected quarters. First, with respect to his plan to leave his wife, Irving quoted the Scripture, 'If any man provide not for his own he hath denied the faith', and went on to assert, 'It seems strange to me that you should leave your wife'. And Emily Cardale cried out, 'To the Word – the written Word! You must not leave her!'[6]

Baxter was amazed that these two – usually strong advocates of the miraculous – should thus reject his revelation and revert to the use of reason and to the dictates of 'the written Word'. He declared:

If a thunderbolt had burst at my feet it could not have created half the pain and agonizing confusion which these utterances have cast upon me.[7]

And his disappointment was made still worse by a letter from Ashley. Ashley had tried to follow out the directions that he baptize the six-weeks-old infant with the Holy Ghost, 'expecting the babe would speak in the Spirit as soon as the ceremony was performed'.

But the infant did not speak. And Baxter, upon learning of this further failure, again told himself he had misunderstood the directions – that they really meant the child would became a prophetess, but at some later date.

Moreover, Baxter did not leave his wife. Despite his confusion he recognized the good sense in the advice given by Irving and Miss Cardale and reluctantly submitted to it.

*　　　*　　　*

Nevertheless, he soon had another revelation! This concerned something even more spectacular; the baptism with fire.

Baxter and Irving had often used the Scripture, 'He shall baptize you with the Holy Ghost and with fire', and Irving had recently declared that 'the baptism with fire' would very soon be experienced. Likewise they asserted the outpouring which was then being witnessed was nothing less than another Pentecost and that all the features of the first Pentecost would be repeated in this second one. And a striking feature of the first Pentecost was

. . . cloven tongues like as of fire, and it sat upon each of them.

Baxter asserted that if they were truly witnessing a second Pentecost these 'tongues like as of fire' *must* be experienced. And before long he was told in a revelation that this startling gift was about to be given and that he was the one who would receive it; at the end of forty days he would be baptized with fire. He did not altogether know what this baptism would be, but he seems to have thought of it as something which looked like fire and that the 'cloven tongues' would sit on him just as they had on the Apostles at Pentecost.[8]

But he also thought of it as ushering in many other blessings. He declared that upon his receiving of this baptism,

. . . power should be given, the sick should be healed, the deaf should hear, the dead should be restored. and all the mighty signs and wonders should appear; apostles and ministers should be ordained, endowed and sent forth to the ends of the earth . . .[9]

With this expectancy before him he returned to his home in Doncaster. By this time his wife had begun to believe the manifestations were of God. Thus their relationship was restored and before long he received, he says:

. . . in the power, a most emphatic declaration, that on the day after the morrow, we should both be baptized with fire. . . .

We were overjoyed . . . and in the fulness of hope and confidence, awaited the day of fulfilment. . . .

The day named arrived, and in the evening an utterance from the power, 'Kneel down, and receive the baptism by fire.' We knelt down, lifting up prayer to God continually.

Nothing however ensued. Again and again we knelt, and again and again we prayed, but still no fulfilment.

Surprising as it may seem my faith was not shaken, but day by day, for a long time, we continued in prayer and supplication, continually expecting the baptism. My wife gradually concluded the whole must be delusion and ceased to follow it. For six weeks, however, I continued unshaken to seek after it, but found it not.[10]

Nevertheless, as a means of explaining away this further disappointment Baxter dropped the idea of literal fire and thought of it only in a figurative sense – an experience in which all sin would be burned out of the soul.

*　　*　　*

Moreover, despite his assertion of being 'unshaken', by this time Baxter, too, was wondering if the whole activity – tongues, the power, prophesying and revelations – might not be a delusion.

Yet there were several factors which helped to maintain Baxter's faith.

1. The lives of the people who believed in the manifestations seemed so earnest and in general so wholesome that he could not easily accept the idea that the activity was false. He wrote:

The supernatural nature of it was so clear, the testimony to Jesus so full – the outpouring of prayer, and, as it seemed to me, the leading towards communion with God so constant in it, that I still could not condemn it, but treated every doubt as a temptation.[11]

2. Irving had taught that this was the way to maintain one's faith. Whenever the slightest doubt arose in the mind, it was to be regarded as coming directly from Satan and must be dealt with just as one would deal with a temptation to sin.

3. Irving had also taught that in adhering to a belief in the manifestations the intellect must be inhibited. To one man he said,

'Abate thy trust in thine own understanding', to another 'Your intellect has destroyed you!' and to still another, 'Keep your conscience unfettered by your intellect.' 'We are not a reasoning people,' he declared, and Mrs. Oliphant speaks of 'the entire devotion with which he had abrogated reason itself'.

Accordingly, recognizing the good fruits of this work, telling himself every doubt came from Satan, and inhibiting the normal functioning of his mind, Baxter inwardly tried to maintain his faith and outwardly continued his practices as a believer in the gifts.

Nevertheless, Baxter's doubts continued. He could not forget the failure of his three major revelations – the Court affair, the command to leave his wife, and the baptism with fire – and although in each case he had got out of his difficulty by assuring himself he had misunderstood the divine directions, the failures stood out in his memory and constantly suggested the whole belief was false.

And beside the three large failures there had been several smaller ones.

He had made numerous prophecies, some forty-six of which had failed. Likewise there had been many attempts to heal the sick and to exorcise demons, and while some had seemed successful, numerous others had failed. Irving had taught that such failures were to be explained by claiming 'the power was hindered by the lack of faith in the person on whom the miracle was to be wrought'. But Baxter was finding it increasingly difficult to accept this excuse and his tendency to disbelief was daily growing stronger.

*   *   *

After some weeks in this condition Baxter was brought to a point of crisis: he met a man by whom his faith was severely shaken and his doubts firmly substantiated.

The man declared that concerning one of the basic doctrines of Christianity, Irving's view was utterly heretical. He mentioned especially Irving's doctrine of 'the sinful substance of Christ', and Baxter, who had simply taken it for granted that Irving was thoroughly sound in all such matters, was shocked. Accordingly, he immediately wrote to Irving, asking whether or not the charge was true.

Irving replied, stating his view and plainly admitting he taught that Christ possessed the same nature as fallen man.

Baxter found it difficult to believe Irving could hold such a doctrine. But, forced to do so by the fact that it came from Irving's own pen, he reasoned out its implications, stating that in this teaching:

... Christ is first abased towards our sinful condition, and we [are] next exalted to be put on an equality with Him: as though Christ had a work to do in making His own flesh holy, and we are enabled to do the same work and make our flesh holy.[12]

The doctrine itself was shock enough for Baxter but its effect went further. He had believed, not only that the manifestations were the work of the Spirit, but also, since they took place under Irving's ministry, that they constituted an unquestionable sign of the Spirit's approval upon Irving, his ministry, his doctrine, and indeed his whole activity.

But now Baxter faced the realization this belief was false. A doctrine such as that which Irving held was in no way approved, but rather was condemned, by the Holy Spirit. And with that realization the aura of the miraculous which, in Baxter's mind had been associated with the tongues, the prophesying, the experience of 'in the power' and the revelations, almost entirely vanished.

Baxter later wrote a *Narrative* in which he reported his experiences in relation to the Irvingite movement and as we read it we see a deep change coming over him at this point.

It shows that his attitude towards the Scriptures became different. As we have seen, he had initially accepted the idea of the gifts largely because several of their features seemed inexplicable on merely human grounds and, like many other people, he assumed that therefore they must be miraculous. He had then been swept along by the seeming supernaturalism of the tongues and the revelations, and in the excitement he had felt no need to look thoroughly into these things and examine them in the light of the Bible.

Now, however, we find him becoming a true student of the Book. The intellect which for months had been inhibited and had substituted mystical impressions for logical thought, now returned to its normal functioning. No longer did he touch a verse here and a verse there, but the man of trained legal mind now engaged in much diligent study, determining the precise definition of words and ascertaining the exact meaning of texts and passages, and in this activity he manifested the same force of reasoning he would have used in arguing a case in court.

And herewith his general outlook became different too. No longer was he burdened with concern about impulses and introspection and with uncertainty as to whether or not he understood the Divine directions in this matter or that. Even the concern about maintaining a constant euphoria was gone and in its place he knew a biblically based assurance and enjoyed a steady peace.

*   *   *

In his later report of his experiences, Baxter pointed out several of the faults which he came to see in the Irvingite practices.

One of his chief complaints related to Irving's demand that the intellect be inhibited. He declared that the Bible stresses, not the *disuse* but the *use* of the mind and he cited such Scriptures as:

'Be not children in understanding . . . but in understanding be men.'
    'The eyes of your understanding being enlightened, that ye may know . . .'
    'That you might be filled with the knowledge of his will, in all wisdom and spiritual understanding.'
    'The Lord give thee understanding in all things.'

And he says that in contrast with these Scriptural statements, Irving

. . . has always striven to put aside the understanding and bring [his] followers into absolute submission to the utterances.[13]

Baxter listed also several other things he considered wrong. The most important was the fact that although all the Prophets claimed to speak by the Holy Ghost, their declarations 'in the power' often contradicted one another. If this was God speaking, he asked, how could He say one thing at one moment and the very opposite at another?

Nevertheless, he still admired Irving and after listing his errors he stated,

. . . with all this, there is so much real candour – real devotedness – real love to God and charity towards all men.

In the matter of the manifestations I believe him to be greatly tried. He cannot shut up his eyes to facts which are daily rising up before him, and yet he is . . . afraid to entertain doubts, and deals with them as temptations. . . .[14]

*   *   *

With his new understanding, Baxter gradually reasoned out his beliefs. As the weeks passed and as he wrote out the several factors which influenced his thinking he came to a definite conviction concerning this whole matter. It was that the various manifestations, despite certain inexplicable features, arose either from psychic activity or from the working of Satan – an attempt, he suggested, by the Devil to discredit the true work of God – and he looked upon the entire development as 'a grand delusion'.

Moreover, he saw the kind of Christian life which is ever seeking spiritual novelties and which places high emotionalism ahead of biblical understanding, as an error. Indeed, more than once he expressed his sorrow concerning the months he had wasted, saying for instance:

Oh! the deep subtilty – the hollowness of our hearts – the awful justice of our God, who, because of the craving after something more than the gentle dew of the Spirit, gave us indeed meat to our lust, by leaving us under a spiritual power, which was supernatural and sweet to the taste, but afterwards wormwood and ashes.'

Surely we have so much of glorious revelation made plain to us, that we can feed upon it in peace and patience . . . and need not to cultivate an unhealthy appetite after crude and novel views, in which we can neither find rest nor edification.[15]

I received a copy of Irving's defence before the Annan Presbytery, and read it with a mixture of admiration and deep pain: the man is of such heroic temper, and of head so distracted.

Poor Dow [Irving's friend] I think will end in a madhouse; Irving will end one cannot prophesy how; he must go on from wild to wilder. This is the result of what once appeared the highest blessing for him: Popularity!

THOMAS CARLYLE, 1833

19

Dismissed from his Church and Deposed from the Ministry

In an earlier chapter we saw that a grievous division had taken place in Irving's church – caused by the speaking in tongues.

On the one side there stood the truly Presbyterian people. Most were of Scottish extraction and many had been with Irving since his days in the Caledonian Chapel. They had been his main helpers in the work of the Church and had borne the chief responsibility in the construction of its new building. Likewise, from this body had come the Church's officials – its elders and deacons.

The other faction was composed largely of newcomers. Some had been attracted by Irving's prophetic speculations, but most by the tongues practices and it was to the latter he was referring when he spoke of having received two hundred new members in the preceding six months. These people had come from various other denominations; few had any knowledge of Presbyterian doctrine or took any real interest in the Church's over-all work and their chief concern lay in the charismatic manifestations.

Between these two factions the antipathy was strong.

This had been the case since the occurrences of the tongues – in the early-morning prayer meetings during the summer of 1831.

But when, in the following autumn, the outbursts of tongues-speaking had taken place during the church services the feelings had become much stronger. The Presbyterians in their love of reverence had denounced the disturbances as a disgrace to the House of God, and the tongues people had replied, declaring that criticism of the manifestations was blasphemy against the Holy Ghost. And thus the hostility had increased and the division had widened.

*　　　*　　　*

Of course, news of the strange goings-on at Regent Square was known throughout the city. The public repeated one scoffing report after another and many a derisive pronouncement was made by the press. For instance, *The Times* remarked editorially:

The great body of Mr. Irving's adherents would probably have remained by him if, in his headlong course of enthusiasm, he could have found a resting-place. They might pardon his nonsense about the time and circumstances of the millennium. They might smile at unintelligible disquisitions about 'heads' and 'horns', and 'trumpets' and 'candlesticks', and 'white and black horses' in Revelations [*sic*]. These things might offend the judgment but did not affect the nerves.

But have we the same excuse for the recent exhibitions with which the metropolis has been scandalized? Are we to listen to the screaming of hysterical women, and the ravings of frantic men? Is bawling to be added to absurdity, the disturber of a congregation to escape the police and treadmill, because the person who occupies the pulpit vouches for his inspiration?[1]

The majority of the Presbyterian members of Irving's congregation were men and women of strong personal dignity and important social standing and we may well imagine their embarrassment in finding their Church thus ridiculed before the public – indeed, in the nation's most prestigious publication.

*   *   *

After the division had prevailed for some months the Trustees decided they could no longer refrain from taking action.

Their first step was an attempt to avoid a crisis. They demanded that Irving forbid the use of the tongues in the church services. He might indulge them at will in the early prayer meeting but he must prohibit them in the church. This was all they asked and they assured him that on this basis peace could be achieved.

But in his certainty that to forbid the tongues at any time would be to silence the Holy Ghost he would not even consider the idea.

Therewith many more of the Presbyterians, seeing nothing ahead but a continuation of the disturbances, left the Church. And one of their number, Archibald Horn, who was both the Senior Trustee and an Elder, not only took his departure, but did so with an open demonstration of his opposition. This Irving reports, saying that on a Sunday morning,

While the Psalm was singing, Mr. Horn came up to the pulpit with a Bible in his hand, and asked me permission to read out of the Scriptures his reason for leaving the church and never entering it more! This I refused, and he went into the vestry, took his hat and went right down the church. Oh, what a fearful thing![2]

Heavy of heart, yet firm in conviction, the Trustees proceeded with the only course of action open to them – that of removing Irving from the ministry of the Regent Square Church. They laid charges before the London Presbytery to the effect that he had allowed the services of the Church to be disturbed, both by persons who were not ministers and by females.

Thereupon the Presbytery ordered him to stand trial before them within a few weeks – 26 April of that year (1832).

It will be remembered that just a year earlier Irving had appeared before the London Presbytery charged with heresy due to his doctrine of 'the sinful substance of Christ'. On that occasion, after hearing the accusation, he had made a powerful defence, and then, scorning his would-be judges, in haughty dignity he had walked out of the Court.

But now matters were different. On the former occasion the Trustees had defended him but now they were his accusers. Moreover, it was evident now that the Presbytery *did* have authority over him and that if they so desired they could remove him from his church. The prospect was a truly humiliating one.

Moreover, a further grief was immediately in store for Irving.

On the morning of the trial a knock sounded at his door. To his amazement the visitor was none other than Robert Baxter, and in his hour of distress Irving heard this man who had formerly been the strongest advocate of the manifestations declare he had come to the conviction that despite their seeming supernaturalism they were all merely a grand delusion!

And with this shattering announcement ringing in his ears and the grievous disappointment weighing upon his heart, Irving went forth to his trial.

The charges against him were heard by the Presbytery and their truth was testified to by witnesses. The trial lasted two days, and for four hours each day Irving defended himself, arguing especially that the outbursts of tongues in his church were in harmony with New Testament practice. But the Moderator held to the charges –

that the outbursts were contrary to Presbyterian doctrine and practice.

The verdict was that which had been expected. It read, in part:

> Therefore this Presbytery, having seriously and deliberately considered the complaint and the evidence adduced . . . do find . . . that the said Edward Irving has rendered himself unfit to remain the minister of the National Scotch Church and ought to be removed therefrom. . . .[3]

Preparations had been made for the celebration of the Communion on the following Sunday and Irving assumed he would be allowed to conduct it as the Church's final recognition of his labours and his last tribute of service to the Church. But the Trustees did not wait till the Sunday and when he arrived for the early prayer meeting on Friday morning he found the gates locked against him.

As we have familiarized ourselves with Irving we have come to know him as a man who, though unswerving in matters of conscience, possessed a very tender heart. He loved mankind and something within him cried out with a need that he be loved in turn. It was with the soul of a true pastor that his affection had gone out to all the flock, and these staunch Presbyterians, who for so many years had been his friends and helpers, had fully shared in that love.

Accordingly, he could not but have suffered a severe wrenching of his whole inner person as he went forth, leaving so many beloved people and quitting the great building in which he had laboured so earnestly.

*　　　*　　　*

But Irving did not go forth alone. Some eight hundred people went with him, and plans were made immediately for the regular carrying on of services. A large room was obtained and services were begun.

Irving soon found, however, that his relationship to this new work was to be very different from what it had been to the old. The Prophets arrogated to themselves virtually a total authority in the management of affairs, and Irving, in the belief that they conveyed the voice of God, had no choice but to submit.

He preached in the rented room, but in this he was under the oversight of the Prophets. Restricted thus in his liberty he undertook also a further labour – one which he assumed would allow him full liberty – the outdoor ministry. He preached in parks and other open places and proved himself able to address very large congregations.

But even in this activity he was not entirely free – people speaking in tongues often interrupted him:

> . . . his is not now the *prophet* voice; by his side or in the crowd near him, is some obscure man or woman to hear whom, when the burst of utterance comes upon them, the great preacher pauses with rapt looks and ear intent; for that utterance, because he believes it to be the voice of God, he has borne 'reproach, casting out, deprivation of everything save life itself' . . . and there he stands, in the unconscious splendour of his humility, offering magnificent thanks when those strange ejaculations give what he believes a confirmation from heaven to the word he has been teaching; a sight, if that voice were true, to thrill the universe; a sight, if that voice were false, to make the angels weep. . . .[4]

After some months in a very unsuitable hall to which they had been directed by the Prophets, the congregation moved into a large picture gallery in Newman Street. In order to prepare it for its new function galleries were constructed and pews and a platform were installed.

The platform, however, was quite unusual – it had six levels. The highest level was for the Apostles and slightly below that was the level for the Prophets. And then in descending order came those for the Elders, the Evangelists and the Deacons. Finally, at the lowest level, was the place for the one whom, in keeping with the designation used in the Book of the Revelation, they termed 'the Angel' or 'the Messenger' – this was Irving.

The explanation for the existence of the highest platform was that one of the Prophets, speaking 'in the power', declared that God intended to raise up Apostles. And a short while later the Prophet was able to state God's designation of the first one: it was the lawyer, J. B. Cardale.

The new organization did not give itself a definite title. In a few years' time it developed into The Catholic Apostolic Church but at this earlier date it was known merely by its location, 'The Church in Newman Street'.

*　　　　*　　　　*

Undoubtedly, after the heart-breaking experiences through which he had passed and the physical strain he was suffering, Irving hoped that somewhere he might find a measure of peace. But instead of repose he now met new trials.

In view of what he considered the terrible wrong done to his friends Campbell, Scott and Maclean, he had written a stinging *Judgment* against the General Assembly of the Church of Scotland.

His thinking seems very difficult to understand, but he charged that the men of the Assembly, since they did not accept his doctrine of 'the sinful substance of Christ', were guilty of rejecting the fundamental truth regarding Christ and therefore of rejecting also the truth regarding God the Father and the Holy Spirit – in short of casting out the very essentials of Christianity.

Moreover, by this time Irving's manner in controversy was showing a further change. Despite his basic graciousness his charges against the Assembly were severely intemperate and his language often became caustic and even bitter.

For months there had been suspicions that Irving's mind was beginning to slip – that together with his undoubted genius there was a measure of mental weakness. And now, since his attack on the Assembly was so virulent and his reasoning so illogical – for a man who believed as he did about Christ, to charge others with apostasy seemed the height of nonsense – in the mind of many those suspicions were confirmed.

Of course, the Assembly did not let Irving's attack and his doctrine go unanswered.

For some months they had considered bringing him into ecclesiastical court and now, moved to action by his statements, they determined to delay no longer. They ordered the Presbytery by which he had been ordained – the Presbytery of Annan – to place him on trial concerning his doctrine of 'the sinful substance of Christ'.

The case was set for 13 March, 1833, and when Irving arrived in Annan he found the town alive with excitement. People poured in from surrounding communities to join with the Annanites in showing their admiration of the district's most famous son and supporting him in his hour of need.

When it was time for the trial to begin (12 noon) the church was packed to the danger point with some 2,000 within and hundreds more without.

The Presbytery was composed of six ministers and the charge was that Irving, in his writings, had 'maintained the sinfulness of the Saviour in His human nature'.

Irving defended himself at great length and with forceful eloquence. But again he was not able to present his doctrine without the appearance of contradiction, saying at one time 'Christ did no sin', but asserting at another that He took upon Himself our sinful nature and possessed the tendencies to sin which all mankind possesses. And his main point, as always, was that Christ was kept from sin only by the indwelling of the Holy Spirit and that we all may equally share that indwelling.

The Court completed its work by seven o'clock and there remained only the final task of the Moderator – that of passing sentence.

But before doing so, in view of the seriousness of the occasion, he called upon the Senior Presbyter to lead in prayer.

At that moment, David Dow, a minister who had accompanied Irving and who was a staunch believer in the manifestations, 'speaking in the Spirit' cried out,

Arise, depart! Arise, depart! Flee ye out, flee ye out of here! Ye cannot pray! How can ye pray? How can ye pray to Christ whom ye deny? Ye cannot pray! Depart, depart! Flee! Flee![5]

The outcry caused a great commotion, especially in the overcrowded galleries.

It was now dusk and the church was lighted by only one candle. One of the Presbyters lifted it aloft and the whole congregation joined him in trying to peer through the semi-darkness to see from whence the sound had come. It was an uncanny situation.

In the midst of the confusion Dow started to leave the church. Irving arose and began to follow, but finding the aisle densely crowded he exclaimed with great vehemence,

Stand forth! Stand forth! What! Will ye not obey the voice of the Holy Ghost? As many as will obey the voice of the Holy Ghost, let them depart![6]

As he strode to the door he again cried out, thundering against what he considered the hypocrisy of such men as these Presbyters leading in prayer! And thus he took his departure.

Back in the church the Moderator pronounced the verdict of the Presbytery. It was that Irving was guilty of heresy and that he was therewith deposed from the ministry of the Church of Scotland.

*　　　*　　　*

Following the trial, in response to the urging of some ministers and many people, Irving remained in the district for some days. He preached out of doors in several places and his ministry almost always drew a large and excited congregation.

But what was the effect of this extraordinary expulsion on Irving himself?

Outwardly he bore up, with his usual unflinching fortitude. But inwardly he was wounded beyond expression. He had found it a cruel enough blow to be debarred from the former delight of his life, the Regent Square Church. But now, to be also deposed from the ministry – a work he had in youth been so earnest to enter, which he had held in such high esteem and in which he had laboured so mightily throughout manhood – this deposition crushed his spirit and, as later events will show, it took from him a basic meaning to life which he was never again to recover.

It was sad to see a lofty mind wasting itself on vague uncertainties ... and a pure and heroic spirit, instead of patiently waiting upon God, hurried on and worn out in the feverish excitement of a restless and bewildering supernaturalism.

ROBERT STORY, 1834

Abide with me; fast falls the eventide;
The darkness deepens; Lord, with me abide!
When other helpers fail, and comforts flee,
Help of the helpless, O abide with me.

HENRY F. LYTE, 1846

20

'The darkness deepens; Lord, with me abide'

One would assume that after undergoing this painful expulsion by the Presbytery in Annan, Irving would receive the warmest encouragement from his people in London.

But such was not the case.

Upon his return to his Church the Prophets gave him to understand that, since his Presbyterian ordination had been revoked, he now had no ministerial status whatsoever. They rebuked him for having preached in Scotland in his unordained condition and, in enforcement of his lack of authority, when an infant was brought to him for 'baptism' they forbade him to perform the rite.

This situation, however, the Prophets proved able to remedy.

One of them, speaking 'in the Spirit' declared Irving could be re-ordained, but that this must be done at the ordering of the Prophets and under the hands of the Apostle, J. B. Cardale.

To this requirement Irving submitted. In an assembly convened for the purpose, Cardale, acting in his Apostolic authority, conferred upon him a new ministerial status and made him again the 'Angel' of the Church. But contrary to all Presbyterian practice Irving was obliged to kneel during the ritual and it was termed, not 'ordination' but 'consecration'.

*   *   *

Moreover, at this very time his family life was plunged into further grief.

His youngest child – an infant a few months old – lay dying. And again in Irving's thinking this was not merely the illness of a beloved little one, but something much more – it was either the cruel affliction of Satan or the righteous judgment of God. Isabella, speaking of the infant's illness, stated, 'The Lord hath punished the child for our sin,' and the sin was that Irving had preached in Scotland in his unordained condition.

Moreover, despite the parents' intercession the child passed away. 'The Lord, in His severity and His goodness,' said Irving, 'hath been pleased to chasten us for our sins ... by removing from us our darling Ebenezer.'

Nevertheless, he also saw a bright spot in the sad event, for he went on to say concerning the infant's last moments,

... when, in faith, I addressed words of godliness to nourish the seed of faith which was in him, his patient heed was wonderful.[1]

The idea of a father 'addressing words of godliness' to a dying infant a few months old, and believing the infant was able to give 'patient heed' to what was said, is surely incredible, and it was this kind of thing which caused Carlyle and others to believe Irving's mind was slipping.

* * *

Moreover, as this year (1833) progressed Irving was confronted by another form of trial.

That is, some who had believed in the manifestations found they could not continue in that belief and had come to the conviction that these things, instead of being miraculous, were merely human.

We have already seen the experience of George Pilkington and Robert Baxter in this regard. Pilkington's publication reporting his days in the Irvingite movement and his reasons for leaving it, had been in circulation for some months, and now there appeared a similar but much longer and more powerful account from Baxter. It bore the title,

NARRATIVE OF FACTS

Characterizing the

SUPERNATURAL MANIFESTATIONS

in

MEMBERS OF MR. IRVING'S CONGREGATION

And Other Individuals In England And Scotland

and

FORMERLY IN THE WRITER HIMSELF

by

ROBERT BAXTER

This was a very heavy blow for Irving. In earlier months he had repeatedly declared that Baxter was being raised up by God as the instrument by which the great outpouring of blessing which would precede the return of Christ was to be administered to the world. Accordingly, to lose him was sorrow enough, but now to be confronted with this widely circulated *Narrative* – an account which made the movement appear fanatical and which spoke of the manifestations as 'a grand delusion' – added extremely to his wounds.

*   *   *

But this was not all. Several other persons experienced a similar loss of faith.

Miss Hall, one of the six original 'gifted ones', declared she had given up all belief in the manifestations. Indeed, she even confessed she had sometimes rehearsed at home the utterances she intended to burst forth with in Church. Her change of mind had been pointed out to Irving during his trial before the London Presbytery, and in answer as to why he had not informed the Court of it he had exclaimed,

She is one of the lambs of my flock – she is carried in my bosom. . . . And shall I bring one of the lambs of my flock, who may have been deluded and led astray, before a public court? Never! Never, while I have a pastor's heart![2]

The essential Irving was probably never more clearly revealed than in these words, 'One of the lambs of my flock', and 'Never! while I have a pastor's heart!' – words spoken even while disappointment was crushing his spirit and darkness was closing in upon him.

Another person who found he could no longer believe in the 'gifts' was Robert Story. When the tongues had first appeared in Scotland, Story had inclined towards the idea that they were supernatural. But as the months went by he studied them carefully and came to the conclusion that, although they contained some features which were not entirely explainable, they were not miraculous. Upon learning of his attitude Irving was deeply disappointed and wrote, saying:

'Oh, Story, thou hast grievously sinned in standing afar off from the work of the Lord. . . . Draw not back, brother, but go forward. The Kingdom of heaven is only to be won by the brave. Keep your conscience unfettered by your understanding.'³

But a still greater disappointment for Irving arose from a similar attitude on the part of A. J. Scott. Though Scott had been foremost in stressing the two-stage concept of the Christian life – 'regeneration followed by the baptism of the Holy Ghost' – he could see nothing truly supernatural in the tongues and the healing practices and he withdrew himself from fellowship with Irving.

And much the same was true of McLeod Campbell and Hugh Maclean. Despite earlier inclinations toward an acceptance of the tongues these men also lost all belief in them and a coldness between themselves and Irving developed.

During 1830 a young man named David Brown had served as Irving's assistant. Thrust thereby into the very midst of the charismatic practices he did his best to believe in them. But witnessing tongues which required so much human inducement and many attempted healings which failed, he found he could not identify himself with these things and ultimately resigned his position. Some time later he happened to meet Irving and said of the incident:

Mr. Irving, after an interval of silence, said, 'Well, Mr. Brown, you have left us.' 'Yes, Mr. Irving; but not, as you know, while there was any shadow of ground to think this work was divine.'

After a moment's pause . . . [Irving] said, with a good deal of suppressed feeling, 'Your intellect, Sir, has destroyed you.' 'Yes, Sir, I confess it; my intellect has done the deed. . . . I am responsible for the use of my intellect and I have used it.'

With his hand held to mine and mine very warmly grasping his, he left me, my feelings very acute, and his, I am sure, the same. And thus ended my connection with this grand man, whose name can never be uttered in my presence without a feeling of love and reverence arising within me.⁴

And David Brown continued to use his intellect. His life produced many scholarly accomplishments, not the least of which was his part in the authorship of the still highly esteemed *Jamieson, Fausset and Brown Commentary.*

*   *   *

But besides the failure of these men and many others to continue to believe in the tongues, Irving faced also the failure of the basic concept concerning the tongues themselves.

The 'gift of tongues', as we saw, was believed to be the ability to speak languages which had not been learned.

This was evident in Mary Campbell (Caird) and her claim to speak Pelew, Turkish and Chinese and her assertion that she was thereby equipped to enter upon foreign missionary service. We have seen the same idea in Irving:

. . . it wanteth [he declared] only the ear of him whose native tongue it is, to make it a very masterful piece of public speech.[5]

Throughout much of 1830 and 1831 this was the belief of most persons in the Irvingite movement, just as during the same period it was the belief of the Mormons in America.

But in 1832 doubts began to be raised among Irving's followers. There was not the slightest evidence that the gift of tongues ever enabled a person to speak another known language and people found they could no longer hold to this theory.

This proved true in the experience of Mary Campbell Caird.

In her intention to become a missionary, accompanied by her husband she went to Europe. But they were immediately forced to recognize her gift of tongues did not enable her to speak any of the languages they came upon. They soon returned to England, and therewith Mary not only dropped the missionary idea completely, but before a few years had passed largely dropped also her belief in the charismatic practices.

Nevertheless, the realization throughout the movement that the tongues were not languages did not mean the loss of the tongues idea itself.

The difficulty was overcome by the assertion that there were two kinds of tongues in the New Testament: (1) those of the day of Pentecost which were languages and (2) those of the Church at Corinth which it was now claimed were merely the ecstatic utterance of incoherent sounds. And since the phenomenon which appeared in Scotland and London did not prove to be this first kind there was now a general acceptance of the idea that it was the second kind which was being experienced.

The realization the tongues were not languages proved a further disappointment to Irving. But he satisfied his own mind in the matter by stating that God had as yet granted only the Corinthian type, that

He had done this merely in order to introduce the restoration of the gifts, and that the Pentecostal type, the languages, would come later.

*   *   *

And Irving met difficulty also concerning the Prophets. He had allowed his whole life to devolve upon the certainty that their utterances came from God, but now circumstances arose which caused him to question this belief.

The first lay in the fact that despite the claim to so high an origin, the utterances were sorely lacking in substance. Very frequently they were no more than 'The Lord cometh!', 'The Lord will speak to His people!' or 'The Lord hasteneth His coming!' Taplin was a chief figure among the Prophets and the following utterance is typical of much that he said:

The Lord hath come down. He is in the midst of you. His eye hath seen, His heart hath pitied the affliction of His people, and He will deliver them. He will not leave a hoof behind.

Utterances had broken out constantly during the service which celebrated the opening of the Newman Street Church. They had begun with the outcry, 'Oh, but she shall be fruitful! Oh! Oh! Oh! She shall replenish the earth!' And after many similar statements they had ended with,

Ah! Sanballat, Sanballat, Sanballat, the Horonite, the Moabite, the Ammonite! Ah! confederate, confederate with the Horonite! Ah! Look ye to it, look ye to it![9]

The utterances were almost invariably of this meaningless nature and they provoked the question, 'Do they really come from God?' It was claimed they were inspired speech, equal in authority to the Scriptures, but people stated that if, in these utterances, God was actually giving a new revelation of Himself, surely they would contain something more substantial – something similar to the Sermon on the Mount, some passages akin to Paul's Epistles or some new Apocalypse superior to that written by John.

And some of Irving's critics declared that if he and his people really believed the utterances constituted a new revelation, they ought to put them into print and bind them up with their Bibles and use and reverence them just as they did any other portion of the Word of God.

But Irving overcame the problem by stating that these utterances, 'like those in the Church at Corinth', were given merely 'for edification' and that they were not related to the realm of the natural understanding. The reader, however, will probably wonder how the utterances cited above – and they are representative of all that have come down to us – could be in any way edifying or helpful.

Difficulty arose also concerning the prophecies.

The Prophets had made numerous assertions 'in the power', foretelling events which they said were then to come to pass. Some of these prophecies came true but many proved false, and the failures left scores of people in the Newman Street Church on the verge of unbelief.

And again Irving rose to the occasion. The difficulty was easily explained – the true prophecies had come from God but the false ones were the work of the Devil!

Yet the matter was not so easily disposed of. Some prophecies had proved half true and half false, and in an effort to deal with the problem it was decided that their origin was twofold – that a Prophet might in one breath be speaking from God, and in the next be uttering under the prompting of Satan.

This was an alarming admission. People were shocked in trying to realize that the utterances which they had believed came directly from God might not be His at all, but might actually be the words of the Devil. They demanded an answer and it was a disappointed and distressed Irving who, seeing no further way out of his difficulties, went before the Church and confessed that much in the utterances might indeed be from Satan and that there was no way of knowing which words were his and which truly came from God.

*　　　*　　　*

And amidst the problems relating to tongues and prophecies there arose also others – these concerned the matter of healing.

Evangelical Christians in general make sickness a matter of prayer, calling upon God for healing, and almost all such persons can testify to instances in which the Lord has heard their cry and has raised the sick to health.

But such Christians also recognize there are times when it is not the will of God to grant healing – when, despite 'the prayer of faith' the sickness continues and sometimes death ensues. Throughout the centuries Christians have accepted such circumstances as the inevitable accompaniment of the life of fallen man and have endeavoured to submit to their trials and benefit from them.

Irving's attitude, however, was different.

He made the statement, 'No Christian ought ever to be overcome by sickness', and it was his belief that the Lord would maintain every Christian in entire health, or, failing that, would grant healing in every case of sickness. All that was needed was sufficient faith and if the healing did not take place, it was because the faith was lacking.

But he also stated that sickness came from two sources: (1) from the cruel working of the Devil and (2) from the righteous judgment of God. And his view included the assertion that 'prayer and faith, and these only, should be employed as the means of deliverance from it'.

We have seen Irving apply these principles in the sickness and death of his two infant sons. The one child died 'to expiate the discords' between Isabella and himself and in the second case 'the Lord had punished the infant' as His judgment upon the parents.

And Irving manifested the same belief when in 1831 there was an epidemic of cholera in Britain. Both Chalmers and Irving took action in the matter. Chalmers declared the disease was caused by unsanitary living conditions and he urged that special care be taken regarding the purification of drinking water and the disposal of sewage. But Irving asserted the disease had been sent by God as his judgment upon the sin of the people and he called for nation-wide prayer and fasting as the only means of deliverance.

The matter of healing played an important part in Irving's ministry.

This had been true ever since the raising up of Margaret McDonald and Mary Campbell in 1830, and although he never conducted healing campaigns or called for the sick to come for healing in his services, the sick were constantly held up before the Lord in prayer. There were numerous instances of failure, but also – as among evangelical Christians anywhere – several in which healing or improvement was evident.

But Irving's people were no healthier than those of any other church and funerals occurred among them in the same proportion as in neighbouring congregations. Moreover, during the preceding eight years Irving had seen three of his children sicken and die and

Mrs. Irving had been unwell during much of their married life. Moreover, now, as 1833 wore on, Irving himself was fast losing the extraordinary health that so long had been his and, although he refused to recognize it, he was becoming the victim of that killing disease: tuberculosis.

*   *   *

How tremendously different were Irving's circumstances now, from what they had been merely five years earlier!

At that time he had been at the height of his success, strong in his liberty, abounding in vigour and listened to by multitudes in both Scotland and England.

But now all was changed.

The Apostles and Prophets dominated the work. All authority rested with them and Irving had become little more than a servant, subject to their utterances and therefore to their commands.

Thus his freedom was gone and with it he had lost all scope for ambition, purpose or endeavour. Life had been robbed of its meaning, he had given up all attempts to write. He preached only when the Prophets wished him to do so and they exerted their control over what he said.

Few men were made for activity so fully as was he, but his great powers of mind and body were now stifled and in his lack of liberty he had become little more than a recluse and seldom ventured far from home.

Irving was not, however, downhearted.

His spirits were constantly buoyed up by the assurance that although thus far he had received none of the charismatic gifts this situation was soon to be vitally altered. He believed God was about to grant him a great outpouring of His Spirit – that he would be suddenly and completely healed, would speak in tongues, and would receive the power to confer the gifts on others by the laying on of his hands and to perform all manner of miracles.

God would thus vindicate him before all his foes and would set him upon a ministry similar to that of the early Apostles. And in this assurance he rested and calmly awaited the day of its fulfilment.

And this was his condition as 1833 drew toward its close.

Edward Irving . . . could I ever forget him, I were the most ungrateful, the worst of men.

His friendship was worth a king's ransom; his aberrations were of the head, not of the heart. His star has disappeared from the galaxy of mighty minds. It is a mournful pleasure to dwell upon what he was.

WILLIAM GRAHAM
a learned and well-to-do Scottish
friend of Irving and Carlyle, 1834

Irving was as the sun in my firmament. His talk so genial, cordial, free-flowing, beautiful and delightful to me; all my meetings with him stand out still as sunlit. A man of noble faculties and qualities; the noblest, largest, brotherliest man I have met with in my life's journey.

THOMAS CARLYLE
a tribute written after Irving's death

21

The Expectancy of Healing, the Continuing Sickness, the Untimely Death

As 1834 opened, despite his optimism Irving was a tired man, weary of mind, sick of body and surrounded by difficulties.

Early in January, however, the Apostles and Prophets commissioned him to undertake a temporary mission in Edinburgh. A man named Tait had recently brought together a company of people there and was seeking to organize them after the pattern of the Newman Street Church. But an evil spirit had entered the work and Irving was to go there for a brief time in order to exorcise the demon and assist in the organizing procedure.

He went, was well received, and was successful in his twofold task.

Upon his return to London, the two Apostles (Drummond had now joined Cardale in this office) went to Edinburgh to complete the work of organization and to ordain Mr. Tait.

During their absence an event occurred which enforced still further Irving's subjection to the Apostles. The Prophet Taplin, speaking 'in the Spirit' gave a command on some minor matter, and Irving, bowing to the belief it was given 'in the Spirit' obeyed it.

But when news of the event reached the Apostles they were incensed. They wrote, rejecting the assertion that the command had been given 'in the Spirit' and sternly rebuking both Taplin and Irving. Therewith Taplin left the Church and did not return for some months. But Irving, despite his blamelessness in the matter, went before the congregation and humbly confessed his error, and the deed he had done thereafter remained in his mind as a grievous sin for which he must expect the judgment of God.

*   *   *

As winter advanced into spring Irving grew steadily weaker.

He was able to exert himself for merely short periods of time and he frequently found it necessary to recline on a couch. When he went out two young ladies, who today would be considered nurses, usually accompanied him.

By this date Carlyle had moved into the house in Cheyne Row which ever since has been a shrine to his memory. He had not seen Irving in many months, and now,

. . . in the middle of a bright May day, [he says] I noticed well down in Kensington Gardens, a dark male figure, which abruptly rose and stalked toward me; whom, seeing it was Irving, I . . . stept out to meet.

It was indeed Irving, but how changed in the two years and two months since I had last seen him! In look he was almost friendlier than ever; but he had suddenly become an old man.

His head, which I had left raven-black, was grown grey, on the temples almost snow-white; the face was hollow, wrinkly, collapsed; the figure, still perfectly erect, seemed to have lost all its elasticity and strength.

We walked some space slowly together, my heart smitten with various emotions; my speech, however, striving to be cheery and hopeful. . . . He admitted his weak health, but treated it as temporary. . . . His tone was not despondent, but it was low, pensive, full of silent sorrow. Once, perhaps twice, I got a small bit of Annandale laughter from him, strangely genuine, though so lamed and overclouded.[1]

A few weeks later Carlyle had dinner with the Irvings. When the visit was over he wrote,

I went away gratified; and, for my own share, glad, had not the outlooks on his side been so dubious and ominous. He was evidently growing weaker, not stronger, wearing himself down, as to me seemed too clear, by spiritual agitations which would kill him, unless checked and ended.[2]

Carlyle then penned a letter to Henry Drummond. He urged that steps be taken to get Irving out of London and into the sunshine of southern Europe for some months. Carlyle considered such action the only way of keeping him from the oppressive conditions of Newman Street and the only means of restoring his health. But feeling the suggestion would be rejected he did not bother to post the letter.

Irving, however, soon called on the Carlyles in their new home. Of course, Jane was there too, and Carlyle reported,

I well [remember] his fine chivalrous demeanour to *her*; and how he complimented her . . . on the pretty little room she had made for her husband and self, and . . . said smiling, 'You are like an Eve, and make a little Paradise wherever you are!'

His manner was sincere, yet with a great suppressed sadness in it. . . . With a fine simplicity of lovingness, he bade us farewell. I followed him to the door. . . . In this world neither of us ever saw him again.[3]

Thus there closed for Jane and Carlyle one of life's most cherished friendships – one they each remembered both joyfully and mournfully throughout their remaining days on earth.

*   *   *

In spite of his longstanding conviction that prayer alone should be used as the means of deliverance from sickness, Irving now visited a physician, Dr. Darling. He placed himself under his care and took his medicines and he seems no longer to have felt that in doing so he was disobeying God.

*   *   *

But now there came for Irving the last great change he was ever to meet.

One of the Prophets, speaking 'in the Spirit', declared it was the command of God that he leave London and go to Glasgow and that God had a great work for him to do there.

Despite his severe illness, this was to him not entirely a distasteful plan. Some years earlier Baxter had prophesied that Irving would some day go to Scotland and there be mightily used of God, and Irving now coupled this promise in his mind with his own assurance that God would heal him and, granting him the whole array of charismatic gifts, would lead him into a powerful and lasting ministry.

With this expectancy before him Irving set out for Glasgow. The month was September and he travelled alone.

He did not, however, go posthaste to his destination. Rather, he planned to move slowly and to take a roundabout trip to the west of England, circling through Wales, returning to England near Liverpool, and then journeying the last stage of the trip by coastal vessel. Such easy travel ought to afford him some relaxation and should do much towards improving his health.

[165]

It did him good to get away from London.

> It is singular . . . to note how, as soon as he emerges from his seclusion in Newman Street, he regains his natural rank in a world which always had recognized the simple grandeur of his character.
>
> Away from that Church, where he rules, indeed, but must not judge, nor act upon even the utterances from heaven, except on another man's authority – where he is censured sometimes and rebuked . . . – the free air of heaven once more expands his forlorn bosom. In the rural places where he goes there is no man 'worthy' who does not throw open his doors to that honoured guest, whose greatness, all subdued and chastened by his weakness, returns to him as he travels.[4]

More than once as he entered a town the cry went up, 'Here's the great Mr. Irving!' Even though his name was treated with scorn by many a Scot and many an Englishman, he seems to have met nothing but welcome and kindness on this trip.

While travelling through Wales Irving wrote almost every day to his wife and children, the oldest of whom, Margaret, was now nine. His letters contain, together with his expressions of affection, descriptions of the beauty of the autumn countryside embellished by scraps of Welsh history. The manner of his writing is simple but fully effective – so much so that it makes one wish he had used the same style in his theological writings.

Yet even here life had its trials.

For instance, in order to travel independently rather than by coach, he bought a horse. But he paid for it with a bank cheque and the next day he was burdened with the thought there might not be enough money in his account to cover it. In his ordination sermon he had warned the young minister against riches. 'Go thou out as poor a man as thou camest in, and let them bury thee when thou diest!', he had charged, and now he was fulfilling his own counsel. Indeed, not only was he poor now, but this had always been his condition.

*　　　*　　　*

His greatest difficulty, however, lay in his illness.

He speaks almost daily of terrible weariness, of a pulse rate of 100 or more and of almost constant fever. He tried to do what he could to improve his condition – one morning he placed a wash basin on the floor of his room, stood in it and poured a large pitcher of cold water over his head and let it run down to his feet. Thereupon he told himself his fever was gone, but before an hour or two had passed he knew it was as bad as ever.

On another occasion he made a most determined effort to secure healing in answer to prayer. He prayed at length with great fervour and in strong faith, and went out of the inn fully assured the divine hand had been laid upon him and he was healed. But again the assurance proved false and he soon realized he was not in the least improved.

Irving's letters to his wife cannot but evoke in the reader an almost tearful sympathy. He speaks of enduring sleeplessness by night and deep weariness by day, together with very frequent suffering and the burning sensations of his fever. His theory of sickness as either the affliction of Satan or the judgment of God must also have burdened his mind, but of this he says nothing at this time and his letters bespeak a quiet submission to his circumstances.

Moreover, notwithstanding his trials he still maintained his hope. He waited for that moment when it would please the Lord to heal him and grant him the gifts, and his faith in this outcome knew no slackening.

*   *   *

Nevertheless, his hope continued to be unfulfilled. As he came to the close of six weeks' travel in Wales he was so weak he was all but unaware of things around him and he could barely keep himself erect in the saddle.

Too feeble to remain alone any longer he wrote for his wife to come and meet him in Liverpool, and upon her arrival she found him, she said, 'looking much worse than when he left home'.

But despite his pitiable state, Irving was determined to set out by vessel on the trip up the coast to Glasgow.

The members of Isabella's family had long been critical of what they deemed Irving's excesses, and now one of her sisters, after describing his condition in a letter, went on to say,

Notwithstanding this they are to sail for Glasgow on Monday. . . . Oh me! it is sad, sad to think of his deliberately sacrificing himself!

Dr. Darling has decidedly said that he cannot, humanly speaking, live over the winter, unless he retire to a milder climate and be entirely at rest. Yet at this inclement season [the third week of October] they proceed northward, and take that cold and boisterous passage too, by way of making bad worse.[5]

Irving and Isabella sailed as planned, and a minister's wife who met them as they reached Scottish soil wrote,

To human appearance he is sinking under a deep consumption. His gigantic frame bears all the marks of age and weakness; his tremendous voice is now often faltering, and when occasionally he breaks forth with all his former feeling, one sees that his bodily powers are exhausted.[6]

And this was Irving's condition as he arrived at Glasgow, hoping to begin the work which would expand into the greatness prophesied by Baxter and which he himself so confidently expected.

But the amount of preaching he did was small. Some of his friends obtained a room in which services could be held; yet he was able to minister there, it appears, on only two Sundays. He preached sitting in a chair, with little strength and very feeble voice.

On the street he needed always a strong masculine arm on which to lean. And after he had been in Glasgow merely three weeks he became so weak that it was necessary for him to remain in bed. He called in a physician, Dr. Rainy, and also consulted another, Dr. Stewart, but there was nothing they could do.

News of the seriousness of his condition brought various relatives to Glasgow – his mother and sister, and Isabella's father, Dr. Martin, and some of her sisters – and in visiting the sick chamber they realized that death was near.

Irving and Isabella alone did not accept this verdict. Despite his steadily worsening condition they were sure the moment would arrive in which the long-expected healing would be granted and he would arise in perfect health – a testimony to all Britain of the reality of the charismatic gifts.

But as the dull, chill month of November drew towards its close, as relatives and friends expressed their despair, and as the days passed in which Irving became still weaker, Isabella almost lost hope. In unspeakable sadness she found herself forced to admit that in this matter also the voice of the Spirit had been misinterpreted and her dear Edward was soon to die.

It was on Thursday, 4 December, 1834, that Isabella thus lost hope. But Irving lingered and the story of his remaining days cannot better be told than already has been done by Mrs. Oliphant.

As the week waned, [she says] the frame which enclosed that spirit, now almost wholly abstracted with its God, died hourly.

He grew delirious in those solemn evenings and 'wandered' in his mind. Such wandering! 'So long as his articulation continued so distinct that we could make anything of his words, it was of spiritual things that he spoke, praying for himself, his church, and his relations.' Sometimes he imagined himself back among his congregation in London, and in the hush of his death chamber, amid its awe-stricken attendants, the faltering voice rose in broken breathings of exhortation and prayer.

Human language has no words . . . for such a divine abstraction of the soul, thus hovering at the gates of heaven.

Once in this wonderful monologue he was heard murmuring to himself sonorous syllables of some unknown tongue. Listening to those mysterious sounds Dr. Martin found them to be the Hebrew measures of the 23rd Psalm – 'The Lord is my shepherd', into the latter verses of which [Irving's] dying voice swelled as [Dr. Martin] took up the wonderful strain, 'Though I walk through the valley of the shadow of death, I will fear no evil.'

As the current of life grew feebler and feebler, a last debate seemed to rise in that soul which was now hidden with God. They heard him murmuring to himself in inarticulate argument, confusedly struggling in his weakness to account for this visible death which all his human faculties could no longer refuse to believe in – perhaps touched with ineffable trouble that his Master had seemed to fail of His word and promise.

At length that self-argument came to a sublime conclusion in a trust more strong than life or death. As the gloomy December Sunday sank into the night shadows, his latest audible words on earth fell from his pale lips. 'The last thing like a sentence we could make out was, "If I die, I die unto the Lord. Amen."'

And so, at the wintry midnight hour which ended that final Sabbath on earth, the last bonds of mortal anguish dropped asunder, and the saint and martyr entered into the rest of his Lord.[7]

They laid the remains in Scotland's most noble place of entombment: the crypt of Glasgow Cathedral. A vast number of citizens thronged to the funeral – among them almost all the ministers of the city and although many had disagreed with him in life they now sincerely mourned him in death.

It is said, and the report is probably true, that a band of young women dressed in white waited in vigil around his tomb, expecting to see him arise from the dead. They believed that God had refused to grant the miracle of healing in order that He might perform the much greater work – that of resurrection – but with the passing of some days they were forced to recognize that their hope was vain.

Mrs. Oliphant closes her account of Irving's death with the words:

There lies a man who trusted God to extremity, and believed in all Divine communications with faith as absolute as any patriarch or prophet; to whom mean thoughts and unbelieving hearts were the only things miraculous and out of nature; who desired to know nothing in heaven or earth, neither comfort, nor peace, nor rest, nor any consolation, but the will and work of his Master . . . a man to whose arms children clung with instinctive trust and to whose heart no soul in trouble ever appealed in vain.[8]

Carlyle, in looking back upon his long friendship with Irving, not only declared he owed much of the success of his literary career to his encouragement, but also stated:

One light shone on him; alas, through a medium more and more turbid: the light from Heaven. His Bible was there, wherein must lie healing for all sorrows. To the Bible he more and more exclusively addressed himself. If it is the written Word of God, shall it not be the acted Word too?

A half man could have passed on without answering; a whole man must answer. Hence Prophecies, Millenniums, Gifts of Tongues, – whereat Orthodoxy prims herself into decent wonder, and waves her Avaunt!

Irving clave to his Belief, as to his soul's soul; followed it whithersoever, through earth or air, it might lead him; toiling as man never toiled to spread it, to gain the world's ear for it – in vain. Ever wilder waxed the confusion without and within. The misguided noble-minded had now nothing left to do but to die. He died the death of the true and the brave. His last words, they say, were: 'In life or death I am the Lord's.' Amen! Amen! . . .

He was as the sun in my firmament. . . . His talk was so genial, cordial, free-flowing, beautiful and delightful to me; all my meetings with him stand out still as sunlit.

But for Irving I had never known what the communion of man with man means. He was the freest, brotherliest, bravest human soul mine ever came in contact with: I call him, on the whole, the best man I have ever . . . found in this world, or now hope to find.

Thus there passed from this life this man of rare greatness and undoubtable goodness, this noble heroic soul, Edward Irving. He died at the age of forty-two, the last twelve years of which had been spent in London, with the final five of this twelve being devoted to the charismatic teachings. Without doubt we may believe that his final words were fulfilled, he died 'unto the Lord'.

'Oh,' [cries one of Irving's biographers,] 'that the whole sad tribe of prophetic pedants and hysterical pietists had gone their own way, leaving him to go his!' Did they not go their own way? And was it their fault that Irving never had a way of his own? Why burden 'the Albury sages' or the crowd of hysterical women which surrounded him, and to whom he gave all too willing an ear, with 'the shipwreck of Irving's genius and usefulness'?. . .

Were it not juster to say simply that this was the particular kind of fire which Irving chose to play with, and that, therefore, this is the particular way in which he burned his fingers. It is altogether probable, being the man he was, that if it had not been in these he would have burned them in some other flames.

BENJAMIN B. WARFIELD
Counterfeit Miracles, 1918

22

Edward Irving: Fore-runner of the Charismatic Movement

The practice of overlooking Irving, which had begun in his lifetime, increased following his death.

Very soon after he died the Church in Newman Street gave birth to a new denomination. It established congregations patterned after itself in various parts of England, on the European continent and in America, and this organization became known as *The Catholic Apostolic Church*. It continued the practice of utterances by the Prophets, together with tongues and healings, but it was particularly characterized by an insistence on the nearness of Christ's return and this teaching was especially fruitful in attracting public attention.

The Newman Street Church had never accorded Irving the position and honour he deserved and in the enlarged body this treatment continued. He was regarded as merely a fore-runner – a kind of John the Baptist – and since that which he had heralded – the Catholic Apostolic Church, replete with the restored charismatic gifts – was now a reality, the role he had played was considered unimportant and he was increasingly forgotten.

Moreover, while Irving had thus left nothing of an institutional nature which worthily commemorated him, the lack was equally present in the realm of literature. His *Works* were published in five volumes, but while there are brilliant paragraphs here and there, much of the rest is very difficult to read and these literary remains probably did his memory more harm than good.

*　　　*　　　*

Mrs. Oliphant's *Life of Irving* served well towards correcting this condition and Carlyle's *Reminiscences* assisted in the same good cause. These authors portrayed him in the greatness of his abilities and the nobility of his character, and though Carlyle did not scruple to manifest something of his faults, the two productions were effective toward keeping his name alive before the public.

But this effect was neither sufficiently wide nor lasting. Many of the derogatory ideas that had arisen in Irving's lifetime remained in circulation and, as the years passed, though some persons held strongly to the image presented by Mrs. Oliphant, numerous others thought of him in the following senses: (1) as a genius, but one whose eccentricities rendered him unwise and even fanatical; (2) as a man whose success had gone to his head and had made him proudly boastful, and (3) as a charlatan who induced hysterical experiences in his hearers and endeavoured to make it appear that he could perform miracles.

And together with these ideas there went the belief that, at least in his later years, Irving's mind had begun to slip. Nor was this concept without a basis, for it came especially from one person best able to express an opinion in the matter – Thomas Carlyle. Notwithstanding the love he had for Irving, Carlyle more than once expressed the feeling that his mind had become affected, and he was saddened, he said, to see even a slight aberration of so fine an intellect. Likewise Chalmers made suggestion to the effect that Irving was natively lacking in a sound mental balance and others indicated a similar view.

Under these conditions there seemed little reason that Irving should be remembered. Accordingly, as the decades passed he faded more and more from the public mind and by the time he had been in his grave for a century the majority of Christians had never so much as heard his name, and even among ministers most could barely identify him.

Thus, the man who in the 1820's had exercised so famous a ministry and had been acclaimed 'by many, many degrees, the greatest orator of the age', had been increasingly neglected and now was largely forgotten.

*   *   *

About the middle of the twentieth century, however, this condition began to change. Circumstances arose which brought Irving into attention and importance again.

By 1950 the Pentecostal Churches of the world were making rapid increase and throughout the years which have followed, that growth has accelerated. Moreover, at the same time the Pentecostal teachings have found widespread acceptance in persons of other denominations, and this development, both within and without the Pentecostal body, is now known as 'The Charismatic Movement.'

This Movement did not arise from any particular knowledge of Irving, but the beliefs held by each have proved very much alike. This fact has been remarked by various charismatic leaders and one of them, Gordon Strachan, has made it the theme of a book, *The Pentecostal Theology of Edward Irving*. Strachan makes mention of this historic likeness and then goes on to say,

> The beliefs and experiences of the various branches of the contemporary Pentecostal Churches are so similar to those of Irving and his followers that one might suspect they had been handed down by word of mouth, or discovered like some Deuteronomy of the Spirit. The fact that there was no collusion between the two movements . . . only emphasizes the power and validity of the comparison.[1]

This new recognition of Irving has been accompanied by efforts to remove the stigma so long attached to his name. Writers have sought to show that the concepts of him as 'eccentric', 'impulsive' and 'lacking in sound judgment' are without foundation, and they have especially rejected the suggestion that he suffered at any point in his life from mental illness. Likewise the attempt has been made to portray him as a consistent thinker, a thorough expositor and a precise theologian.

Accordingly, among numerous charismatic people there has developed the realization that here was one, a century and a half ago, who held the same views as they hold today. Thus there is a steadily increasing interest in him, his beliefs and his practices, and together with a warm admiration there is a growing recognition of him as 'the Forerunner of the Charismatic Movement.'

*　　　　*　　　　*

Nevertheless, while we rejoice in this well-deserved recognition we must not let the instructions and warnings inherent in Irving's experiences pass by unnoticed.

Throughout this book the attempt has been made simply to present the facts of his life and let them speak for themselves. But we do well, before we leave the study, to review some of those facts and let them repeat their lessons.

First, we recall Irving's willingness to believe that new revelations were being given by God. During his days as a Presbyterian he had believed that God had provided a completed revelation in the Scriptures and there was no such thing as even a thought of something further in that regard.

But when he heard the utterance in a tongue and its interpretation into English, he was dogmatic in his assurance that this was the very voice of God. He believed that the words spoken 'in power' were inspired speech and that they constituted a new revelation equal in authority to the Bible.

Herein lies a most important lesson for today. Not only did the belief in new revelation bring on the ruin of Irving's career, but it will mean the ruin of the faith of any who accept it. The idea of further revelation not only robs the Scriptures of their finality and therefore of their authority, but also strikes at the very foundations of Christianity. It would allow every man to become a law unto himself and to 'do that which is right in his own eyes', and would leave mankind without a definite 'Thus saith the Lord!' on any subject.

Of course, many of the charismatic people today stand as firmly as anyone in defence of the Scriptures. But Irving's experience points out the grave danger of accepting even the possibility of 'new revelation' and indicates the necessity for all who believe The Book stoutly to reject all professed further revelations whether they be in visions or dreams or the hearing of voices, and to hold solely to the finished revelation, the written and inerrant Word of God.

*   *   *

Secondly we recall Irving's ideas regarding sickness and healing.

We saw his statement that 'bodily disease is the direct infliction of Satan, and that therefore faith and prayer, and these only, should be employed as the means of deliverance from it'. But he believed that sickness could also come as the judgment of God and he looked upon the illness and death of three of his children as both Satan's infliction and God's judgment in his life.

Illness and trouble were to Irving evidences of Divine displeasure. Yet not only was the theory unscriptural, it was also cruel – cruel to himself and likewise to others suffering ill-health or tragedy.

Moreover, Irving's view that healing was available in every instance of sickness was equally false. Many a victim of disease must have found his pain increased by the feeling he was either suffering the angry judgment of God or the cruel wrath of Satan – especially when healing did not come and he lingered in agony.

Furthermore, if ever a man was certain he would be healed it was Irving in his last sickness. But as we have seen, the miracle of healing was denied, his life steadily ebbed away and he came down to an untimely death.

And we of today may well be both instructed and warned by the unscripturalness of Irving's belief and its sad effect in his own darkest hour.

*   *   *

Thirdly, lessons are to be learned from the general failure of Irving's career.

At the close of his first year in London he stood on the pinnacle of fame. He was yet merely thirty-two and it seemed he could not fail to go on to a life of the greatest success. This man, it appeared, must surely attain a fulness of magnificent accomplishment and, dying, go down in history among the most noteworthy ministers of all time.

And had he continued to hold his Presbyterian beliefs such undoubtedly would have been the case.

But, as we have seen, he was led by A. J. Scott to expect the restoration of the charismatic gifts. Likewise, under Scott's influence he accepted the idea of two definite stages in the Christian life, the first that of regeneration and the second that of the baptism with the Holy Ghost, this latter experience evidenced by 'speaking in tongues'.

Thereafter the idea that there are two distinctly different levels of the Christian life held a foremost place in Irving's thinking. Believing, as he did, that only those who spoke in tongues had received the baptism with the Holy Spirit, he regarded these persons as on the higher level and therefore as much superior in spiritual power. All others he looked upon as on the lower level and as spiritually inferior.

The chief effect of this belief was that it brought Irving into subjection to the Prophets. Since they spoke in tongues he conceded to them a position far superior to his own, and thereafter his life came under their control. The Irving we have seen in the last two years of his life, a recluse, robbed of his liberty and with little ambition to write or be active, was the result of his acceptance of the Prophets and their gifts.

Thus a life which could have been so great a success came down to disappointment and failure.

This outcome seems all the more regrettable as we view Irving in contrast to various other men of his century. We think, for instance, of such fellow Scots as Chalmers, the Bonar brothers (Horatius and Andrew), Robert Murray M'Cheyne and David Livingstone; then, too, of the Englishman C. H. Spurgeon, and of George Müller, the German who maintained the orphan houses in England. These men are true examples of a holy life and the enduement with 'power from on high,' and the suggestion that such persons as Irving's Prophets were their spiritual superiors is manifestly foolish.

Yet these men, and hundreds of others like them, believed that the presence of the Holy Spirit is an integral part of regeneration. Being 'born again' they were indwelt by the Spirit of God, and for them the Christian life was one of steady increase in being 'filled with the Spirit', and a daily growing 'in grace and in the knowledge of our Lord and Saviour, Jesus Christ'.

The difference between the spiritual triumphs of these men, resulting from their beliefs, and the failure experienced by Irving as a result of his views, stands out plainly, and provides clear lessons and strong warnings for both the Charismatics and non-Charismatics of today.

*   *   *

In reading this account of Irving, various readers may have found themselves puzzled concerning his conversion. Admittedly he sometimes spoke critically of evangelicalism and, in general, he held to a belief which can barely be distinguished from 'baptismal regeneration'. Nevertheless, throughout his beliefs, despite their confusion and contradiction, there is often to be found a basic acceptance of the Gospel. Moreover, as we have seen, his life frequently manifested the fruits of true Christianity, and did so in rich abundance, and we must conclude that, notwithstanding his lack of clear statement in the matter, beyond all doubt he was a converted man.

As we come, then, to the close of these hours spent in the company of the magnificent but tragic Irving, we may best take our farewell as we see him reflected in the words of Robert Murray M'Cheyne. Upon learning of Irving's death, M'Cheyne, who was a theological student at the time, wrote in his *Diary*:

I look back upon him with awe, as on the saints and martyrs of old. A holy man, in spite of all his delusions and errors. He is now with his God and Saviour, whom he wronged so much, yet, I am persuaded, loved so sincerely.

Notes

Abbreviations:

CR   Thomas Carlyle, *Reminiscences*. Dent ed., 1972
CC   Thomas Carlyle, *Correspondence*
Ol   Mrs. Oliphant, *The Life of Edward Irving*, 1864 ed.
St   Robert Story, *Memoir of the Life of the Rev. Robert Story*
BN Robert Baxter, *Narrative of Facts Characterizing the Supernatural Manifestations in Mr. Irving's Congregation*

1. *A Happy Boyhood*
   1. CR 172
   2. CR 175

2. *Teen-aged University Student*
   1. CR 179, 180

3. *The Hard Road to The Ministry*
   1. CR 38, 39
   2. Crabbe Robinson, *Diary, Reminiscences and Correspondence*, London, 1869, 488

4. *Assistant to Dr. Chalmers*
   1. CR 195
   2. Ol 108

5. *The Sudden Burst into Fame*
   1. Ol 69
   2. George Gilfillan, *Gallery of Literary Portraits*, London, 1846, Vol. 2
   3. William Hazlitt, *The Spirit of the Age*, London, 1825

6. *Irving's Reaction to Popularity*
   1. Ol 73
   2. Ol 74
   3. Irving, *Orations*, London, 1823, IX

7. *A Unique Friendship: Irving and Coleridge*
   1. *The Collected Works of S. T. Coleridge*, ed. Katheleen Coburn, Princeton University, 1976, Vol. 10, p. 143

2. CR 251
3. W. Hanna, *Memoirs of Thomas Chalmers*, Edinburgh, 1849–1852, Vol. III, p. 160
4. Here cited from A. L. Drummond, *Edward Irving and his Circle*, (James Clarke & Co., Cambridge), 1934, p. 68
5. Ol 96
6. Ol 98

8. *Marriage*
   1. CC Vol. 2, 409
   2. J. A. Froude, *Thomas Carlyle*, Vol. 1, 481, 125
   3. Cited from A. L. Drummond, *Edward Irving and his Circle* (James Clarke & Co., Cambridge), 1934, 92
   4. *Dictionary of National Biography*, Art. 'Irving'

9. *Babylon and Infidelity Foredoomed*
   1. Ol 104, 105
   2. Ol 107
   3. BN 129
   4. *Fraser's Magazine*, Edinburgh, 1831, No. 61
   5. Hazlitt's *Works*, Vol. 2, 285
   6. *Irving's Preliminary Discourse 'on Ben Ezra'*, 5, 6

10. *Death Strikes in the Irving Household*
    1. CR 255
    2. Ol 112
    3. Ol 113
    4. Ol 150

11. *Irving at his Best – and less than his Best*
    1. Irving's *Ordination Charge* is published in full in his *Works*, Vol. 1, 527–540
    2. Ol 209
    3. Ol 209
    4. Ol 209

12. *Accused of Heresy – 'Christ's Sinful Flesh'*
    1. Ol 221, 222
    2. *Works*, IV, 526–559
    3. A. A. Hodge, *Outlines of Theology*, New York, 1894, 380
    4. *Fraser's Magazine*, January, 1832

13. *Irving at the Height of his Career*
    1. Ol 229

2. Ol 230
3. Ol 231

14. *The Gathering Storm*
    1. Ol 243
    2. Ol 259
    '3. Ol 263
    4. Ol 266

15. *'The gift of tongues' in Scotland*
    1. St 194
    2. St 194
    3. St 195
    4. Ol 275, 276
    5. Ol 276
    6. St 198
    7. St 202, 203
    8. St 204
    9. St 230, 231
    10. St 231

16. *'The gift of tongues' in London*
    1. *Fraser's Magazine*, January, 1832
    2. Ol 297
    3. Edward Miller, *The History and Doctrines of Irvingism*, London, 1878, 62, 63
    4. Miller, 62
    5. Ol 318
    6. Ol 328, 329

17. *The Gifts in Action*
    1. George Pilkington, *The Unknown Tongues Discovered to be English, Spanish and Latin*, London, 1831
    2. Pilkington, *The Unknown Tongues*
    3. Miller, *Irvingism*, 72
    4. Anti-Cabala, here cited from A. L. Drummond, *Edward Irving and His Circle*, (Cambridge), 1934, p. 166
    5. CC Letter of 20 October, 1831
    6. Ol 320
    7. Pilkington, 10
    8. Ol 324, 325
    9. Ol 331

18. *Robert Baxter and the 'Baptism with Fire'*
    1. BN 4, 5

2. BN 16
3. BN 17
4. BN 24, 25
5. BN 39, 40
6. BN 50
7. BN 50
8. BN 64
9. BN 66
10. BN 90, 91
11. BN 96
12. BN 109
13. BN 127
14. BN 130
15. BN 139

19. *Dismissed from his Church and Deposed from the Ministry*
    1. Ol 330
    2. Ol 333
    3. Ol 366
    4. Ol 370
    5. Ol 395
    6. Ol 395

20. *'The darkness deepens; Lord, with me abide'*
    1. Ol 399
    2. Ol 364
    3. St 227
    4. W. G. Blaikie, *A Memoir of David Brown*, London, 1898, 41, 42
    5. Ol 329
    6. Ol 382, 383

21. *The Expectancy of Healing, the Continuing Sickness and the Untimely Death*
    1. CR 302
    2. CR 304
    3. CR 305
    4. Ol 409
    5. Ol 422
    6. Ol 423
    7. Ol 426, 427
    8. Ol 428

22. *Edward Irving, Fore-runner of the Charismatic Movement*
    1. Gordon Strachan, *The Pentecostal Theology of Edward Irving*, Darton, Longman and Todd, London, 1973

Index

Index